POETRY RE

A U T U M N   1 9 9 8   V O L U M E

EDITOR PETER FORBE
PRODUCTION STEPHEN TRO
ADVERTISING SOPHIE JEPSON SUBSCRIP

CONTENTS

LONDON MAGAZINE

FICTION * MEMOIRS * CRITICISM * POETRY

CINEMA * ARCHITECTURE * PHOTOGRAPHY

THEATRE * ART * MUSIC

'A fantastic magazine whose place in the history of 20th century literary life grows ever more secure and significant' – *William Boyd, Evening Standard*

Each issue contains over 50 pages of poems and reviews of poetry.

Forthcoming features

Herbert Lomas on Kenneth Allott & Ronald Bottrall

Georg Trakl & Li He: poets of decadent empires

Simon Carnell on Ted Hughes

John Clare and the Bikers

Michael O'Neil, Andrew Waterman, Andrew Johnston

on recent poetry

Subscriptions:
£28.50 p.a. (six issues) to 30 Thurloe Place, London SW7

Single copies £5.99 from discriminating bookshops

POETRY REVIEW
SUBSCRIPTIONS
Four issues including postage:

UK individuals £23
Overseas individuals £31
(all overseas delivery is by airmail)
USA individuals $56

Libraries, schools and institutions:
UK £30
Overseas £37
USA $66

Single issue £5.95 + 50p p&p (UK)

Sterling and US dollar payments only. Eurocheques, Visa and Mastercard payments are acceptable.

Bookshop distribution:
Signature
Telephone 0161 834 8767

Design by Philip Lewis
Cover by Stephen Troussé

Typeset by Poetry Review.

Printed by Grillford Ltd at 26 Peverel Drive, Bletchley, Milton Keynes MK1 1QZ
Telephone: 01908 644123

POETRY REVIEW is the magazine of the Poetry Society. It is published quarterly and issued free to members of the Poetry Society. Poetry Review considers submissions from non-members and members alike. To ensure reply submissions must be accompanied by an SAE or adequate International Reply coupons: Poetry Review accepts no responsibility for contributions that are not reply paid.

Founded 24 February 1909
Charity Commissioners No: 303334
© 1998

THE POETRY SOCIETY

EDITORIAL AND BUSINESS ADDRESS:
22 BETTERTON STREET, LONDON WC2H 9BU

telephone   **0171 420 9880**
fax   **0171 240 4818**
email   **poetrysoc@dial.pipex.com**
website   **http://www.poetrysoc.com**

ISBN 1 900771 10 1
ISSN 0032 2156

Funded by
THE ARTS COUNCIL OF ENGLAND

FANFARE FOR THE COMIC MUSE

PETER FORBES ON COMIC AND TUFF-LITE POETRY

The Funny Side: 101 Humorous Poems

Edited by Wendy Cope,
Faber, £7.99
ISBN 0 571 19651 9

AUDEN SAID: "A great many people dislike the idea of poetry as they dislike over-earnest people, because they imagine it is always worrying about the eternal verities". He was a champion of light verse, writing it with great distinction and editing *The Poet's Tongue* (1935), a famously democratic anthology of its day for young people. In *Letter to Lord Byron* he elevated light verse to high art. But when does light verse become comic? Is wit funny? Can humorous verse avoid the silly-clever, self-satisfied, and often disgustingly reactionary twitterings of the Chesterbelloc kind? Light verse of the Auden variety, that is verse which can move nimbly about subjects great and small, always grounded in sceptical humanism, is in remarkably good health, which makes National Poetry's Day's choice of comic verse a happy one.

As John Whitworth shows in his table on p.23, poets have always been divided into the jokers and non-jokers. I suspect there is no bridging this gap. If you cling to Geoffrey Hill's every utterance with the raptness of *Agenda* magazine it's unlikely you'll approve of serious poets like Fenton or Fuller who often resort to playfulness and even nonsense.

Wendy Cope was the obvious choice for Faber's National Poetry Day effort: a funny poet grounded in the seriously light tradition of Auden and Ewart. She is a connoisseur of dry wit and bathos: belly laughs and inanity are not her thing at all. I think an acid test of whether you'll like her selection is Auden's brief 'Note on Intellectuals':

> To the man-in-the-street, who I'm sorry to say
> Is a keen observer of life,
> The word Intellectual suggests straight away
> A man who's untrue to his wife.

It reminds me for no very good reason of a graffito in the Gents loo of the old, British Library:

'Everything passes, nothing remains' – Aristagoras
'Nothing passes, everything remains' – Constipagoras

The point is that, in each case, to like them you have to have both a taste for philosophy and a love of debunking high-flown pretensions. The man-in-the street invoked in Auden's poem wouldn't find it interesting; nor would an ascetic intellectual like Geoffrey Hill. Which narrows it down somewhat, but since it includes me, it's all right.

The Funny Side is a canny collection, including many of the canonical crowd pleasers (even down to Chesterton and Belloc, but I didn't really think she would leave them out), but it's especially sharp in its contemporary pearls: Fenton's 'The Skip' in which he picked up "a decent, an authentic life", Fleur Adcock's classic of self-reproach 'Things', Kit Wright's Tunbridge Wells Western 'How the Wild South East Was Lost', Glyn Maxwell's all-purpose 'Deep Sorriness Atonement Poem'.

In her intro, Wendy Cope wishes that the term "light verse" could be abandoned: "the word 'light' seems to imply that a poem can't be funny and serious (weighty) at the same time". Well, obviously it can be I'm not sure she's right about "light". Italo Calvino, than whom no one was more seriously erudite, loved the word "light", meaning quicksilver, nimble, ethereal. "Light" verse, in this sense, is alert to its own vulnerability, the antithesis of pompous, puffed up, priggish.

James Fenton's 'In a Notebook' or Kit Wright's 'I Found South African Breweries Most Hospitable' would not have been possible if the writers hadn't also written seriously funny poems like 'The Skip' and 'How the Wild South East Was Lost', respectively.

Incidentally, Kit Wright has a poem here which sends up Roy Orbison's 'Only the Lonely' and shows the comic muse still finding its *données* in the usual unlikely places: "Only the lonely / Know the way you feel tonight? / Surely the poorly / Have some insight? // ...And lastly the ghastly / Know the way you feel tonight".

THE SONNET HISTORY

JOHN WHITWORTH
SOMETHING

"But what happens if I get old or something?"
Asked the most famous poet on the planet
Really wanting to know. What happens if
My face collapses like a pomegranate
And nothing works to keep my pecker stiff
And Peter doesn't love me? It's a dumb thing,
A glum, thing, numb thing, if you get old or something.

"People will always like you. You're a nice person."
A good answer, most of us would agree,
From a good shrink, the famous poet's friend.
It handed him permission to be free,
And people did always like him. If near the end
Poor Peter got shot to hell, some things do worsen
When you're old or something, for even the nicest person.

JOHN WHITWORTH
THE WAR POETS

"What poems do I like? Do you mean for *fun*?"
I nod. She frowns, "We do First World War stuff".
"No nightingales or daffodils?"
                                    "No, none".
The young today must take their poems tough.

Those real and relevant War Poets died –
Owen and Brooke and Rosenberg – and some
Let off the dying, got screwed up inside.
Their Muse went mad, or blind, or deaf, or dumb.

This peaceful poet's done his stint. And she,
To show me out, has dodged her English class.
She frowns again, "I hate War Poetry!
Goodbye". Her sandals shimmer through the grass.

Where'er she walks the insistent flowers spread,
And choirs of songbirds flutter round her head.

JOHN WHITWORTH
THE VOICE OF THE BARD

– Protestant or Catholic?
– I'm Jewish
– Protestant Jewish or Catholic Jewish?

I write these lines in praise of Seamus Famous
Who scooped the Nobel Prize and rightly so.
There's not a lot big Seamus doesn't know
About our Craft. An Oxford Prof, the same as
Auden and Graves, he is no ignoramus
But wears his learning lightly, with a show
Of Irish charm that's every inch the pro
And never gets reptilian or squamous.

The rest of us are tempted and we fall:
We hone the edge of literary malice;
We join the politicians' hokey-cokey.
But Seamus, in a voice as thick and smoky
As Irish Malt, rejects the poisoned chalice,
Smooth and urbane as any cardinal.

Reprinted from *From the Sonnet History of Modern Poetry* (Peterloo, £7.95, ISBN 1 87147 179 6),
published for National Poetry Day.

Cartoon Capers

by Paul Groves

JOHN WHITWORTH
& GERALD MANGAN

From the Sonnet History
of Modern Poetry

Peterloo Poets, £7.95
ISBN 1 87147 176 1

THOSE FAMILIAR WITH *Poetry Review*'s Sonnet History will not be surprised to learn that John Whitworth and Gerald Mangan are having their efforts published by Peterloo. Mangan's fine line drawings have won many admirers and have nicely counterpointed Whitworth's witty and acerbic verses (some might even say outshone them). They have given a welcome lift to pages which can seem on occasion overearnest.

Earnestness is not a quality you associate with Whitworth. He is as happy to send himself up as to send his subjects up. To those in a hurry he can seem a stringent satirist; on closer inspection he is fairly diffuse. His task is helped and hindered by his parameters: "They are all sonnets according to me". He appears Cervantic, tilting at windmills, or a dyed-in-the-wool malcontent pitching at assorted Aunt Sallies and sacred cows with boyish bravado. It is not always easy to see where he stands: satire can demolish the well-meaning along with the puerile and in so doing emasculate itself, reducing it to the medium of cheap laughs and unconsidered jibes. Whitworth inhabits a loftier zone, though only just. "I feel I've hit on something here", he says about a sonnet in which he claims, as Jake Strugnell, "Frankly, most Women's Poems are a joke".

The book challenges you to take him seriously with a pinch of salt. Whitworth has the best (he can make outrageous comments without having to justify himself) and the worst of both worlds (he can make perceptive *aperçus* without anyone believing him). He is prepared and content to run this risk, though it does leave him in the middle of no-man's-land with his critical trousers around his ankles – which demonstrates that if you try to have it both ways you end up having it neither.

Themes bubbling below the surface include Scottishness vs. Englishness, his lack of money, and a ghostly sense of religion (is he a lapsed Presbyterian?). He uses the full sump-estate vocabulary – "nutter", "yids", "filthy rich", "bloody Yanks", "wise up, wankers"...; and rhymes "Beau Brummel" (sic) with Craig Raine's "sonnet to his bumhole". There's a Lallans nod towards 'Ozymandias': "LOOK OAN MA WURKZ, YI BASTUDZ, AN DESPAIR!" and some anti-Hibernian paranoia: "One would like to believe it was an Irish plot or a publisher's plot or something. But there just seem to be a lot of Irish poets about the place". His playful xenophobia phases into over-statement when he says: "Poets are criminals, or drunk, or loony / Or (which is much the same) apart and holy". Into which category would Whitworth place himself?

Dennis Potter was variously called "a rancid puritan" and "the inverted Savonarola of a faithless age". Elements of these extreme states are to be found in Whitworth's dithyrambs against all and sundry. Yet is he merely acting Devil's advocate? When he compares Simon Armitage with George Herbert one's parallelometer whirls alarmingly.

With a few exceptions, the sonnets transcend doggerel. At their best they have vigour and a touch of enchantment. Contrast the expendable 'Mrs Parker and Stevie' with the achieved 'The Wild Good Lookers' – or the disappointingly slight 'Concrete and Clay' with the professional and amusing 'Hard Ham And Old Al' – and you'll gauge Whitworth's range. In 'Poetry With Balls', a subtle title if ever there was one, he says in the foot-note (every poem has one): "'Which Twin Has The Toni?' was an advertising slogan about a shampoo or a home perm, I forget which". This air of extem-poraneousness often threatens to undermine the volume. Had he done his homework he would have avoided an admission of ignorance. "Which twin has the Toni?" was a 1950s slogan for a home perm. See the *Bloomsbury Dictionary of Popular Phrases* by Nigel Rees, available at all good bookshops.

Whitworth and Mangan fill a space in the market if not a need. They inhabit the world of W. S. Gilbert and Bill Greenwell, Hilaire Belloc and Stanley Sharpless, G.K. Chesterton and Katie Mallett, though not "Jolly Jim Fenton" who became a millionaire "And made it out of writing verse, so there!" If you can live with Whitworth's tongue-in-cheekness, this book could be for you; if you easily tire of deciding when a clown is actually being serious you would be better off with verse which does not so egregiously dissimulate.

All Sit-down Comedians Now

GRIFF RHYS JONES ON HIS ANTHOLOGY, *THE NATION'S FAVOURITE COMIC POEMS*

WHAT IS A COMIC poem? How do you decide? What criteria could you possibly employ? Well, soon the nation will decide and, to help you in your choice, I have made up my own selection of likely candidates. It wasn't easy because, alas, not all comic poems are funny, particularly those that try to be. But, as you wander through this collection, I hope you'll be tickled. You will also find that poets high and low, famous, great even, have managed to write some pretty funny stuff on the side, even if our leading contributor is, nonetheless, Anon.

Happily, there is a type of writer who, if often shown the door in other anthologies, has the run of the house here. These are the masters of their craft, the wizards of the unexpected rhyme: the Comic Poets. Perhaps it was the freedom to write nonsense, inflicted so successfully on children by Edward Lear and Lewis Carroll, that opened the way to the gloriously silly stuff. (Although I suspect that *Punch* had a lot to do with it.) Anyway, it is good to see those old nags Hilaire Belloc and Harry Graham coming round the track again. The nursery mood may not be very elevating, but it can be pretty funny.

One of my personal favourites is this little verse by the American wit Gelett Burgess, which was first published in the 1890s:

> I never saw a Purple Cow,
> I never hope to see one;
> But I can tell you, anyhow,
> I'd rather see than be one.

Some years later he wrote again:

> Ah yes! I wrote the 'Purple Cow' –
> I'm Sorry, now, I Wrote it!
> But I can Tell you, Anyhow,
> I'll Kill you if you Quote it!

Poor man. For all I know he designed lunatic asylums or walked backwards to the North Pole. Today all that survives of his verse is this piece of doggerel. I suppose he would have been mortified to find it still doing the rounds.

Mind you, all good jokes are a sort of poetry, aren't they? Gagsmiths know the value of the *mot juste*, the necessity of rhythm and, er, of course, that

timing thing. It should come as no surprise that poetry returns the compliment. Puns, wordplay, hidden meanings and the wrong-footing of cherished notions: it's the very stuff of verse. But jokes eventually die off. Funny poems go on. (On and on, some of them. Lewis Carroll could prolong the hilarity through many a now-forgotten stanza.)

I once recited Robert Service's stirring 'The Cremation of Sam McGee' (not short, but sublime) at a fund-raising event and a woman came up to me afterwards. She voluntarily "did" half of 'The Shooting of Dan McGrew' while I queued for my coat, and continued while I walked down a flight of steps and got into my car. She may be doing it still, for all I know. People *will* carry around rhyming saws and useful epithets for the purpose of bringing them up at appropriate moments. Some of them are here. If you lack these essentials to good conversation, feel free to pinch a few.

Mind you, if you are going to plagiarize, it is as well to remember that brevity is the soul of other people's wit. For my own purposes, I find Sir Walter Raleigh very useful. He wrote a series of verse observations to an artist friend, on postcards. (This is a later Walter Raleigh, by the way. Not the one with the inflatable short trousers and the potatoes.)

> I wish I loved the Human Race;
> I wished I loved its silly face; ...
> And when I'm introduced to one
> I wish I thought *What Jolly Fun!*

Cynics often join me in cackling at this. "It sums it all up, eh?" Though to be fair, it was written about some sorry-looking old trout at a garden party and was meant as criticism. Anyway, my point is I always edit the middle couplet out for efficiency. You can find the full version on page 141 of the book.

It is a challenge to try to be profound and laugh-out-loud funny at the same time. This is why poets of wit, invention and style, like John Donne and Alexander Pope, at whom professors may chortle and teachers hoot, are minimally represented in this anthology.

It is also a pity that certain poets so deeply

profound as to be utterly asinine are not here either. Is there anything in the whole of literature more amusing than William Wordsworth struggling to elevate the commonplace?

> Spade! With which Wilkinson hath tilled his lands.
> ('To the Spade of a Friend')

Or how about this, from one Lillian Curtis, who wrote, in all seriousness:

> I loved the gentle girl,
> But oh, I heaved a sigh,
> When first she told me she could see
> Out of only one eye.

A victim of the measles, apparently. But these are bad poems which are unintentionally funny, and they need their own collection. (*The Nation's Favourite Terrible Poems* perhaps?)

There is also a lot of recent writing here. After all, the nation's favourite modern poem was a funny one. 'Warning' by Jenny Joseph is naturally in the running again. But so are poems by Wendy Cope, Pam Ayres, Roger McGough and Roald Dahl. So are ones by John Hegley and E. J. Thribb, the myth-ical contributor to *Private Eye*.

Poets these days have all become sit-down comedians. Almost everybody from Allen Ginsberg to Brian Patten seems to get off on the "wry look at the way we live now".

But the funniest poem? Well, we shall have to wait until the votes are counted. As old television schedulers say: "There's no accounting for public taste". And there are some rum doings here.

Altogether, however, this is a testament to the power of poetry to move us in the chest-heaving sort of way. (Laughter and tears, they're never very far apart, are they governor? Is there a more moving love poem in the English language than 'The Courtship of the Yonghy-Bonghy-Bò'?) Comic poems, I vow, are a great popular means of expression. You only have to sit in the lavatories at Kings Cross station to understand that. It will be fascinating to see what gets the popular vote on the night.

Remembered, half-remembered, beloved, cherished or written on tea towels, here are some of my favourite comic poems.

Reproduced by permission of BBC Books from *The Nation's Favourite Comic Poems*.

Mirth of Nation's

by Sophie Hannah

The Nation's Favourite Comic Poems
Edited by Griff Rhys Jones
BBC Books, £5.99
ISBN 0 56338 451 4

THE TITLE OF this book puts pressure on the poems in it. You start to read them with the preconception that they will be not merely funny, but the funniest of the funny. It's very hard not to approach them with high expectations and, when you come across one that doesn't make you smile, let alone laugh, it's difficult not to resent it for failing to live up to the promise the anthology title makes on its behalf.

Part of what I like most about funny poems is when they take me by surprise. I like to read them with no expectations and discover, almost by accident, that they make me laugh. If I know I'm expected to be amused beforehand, I'm less likely to be, although this could just be me being contrary.

In a way there's no point in saying this, though, because I know full well that the theme of National Poetry Day this year is humorous poetry, and I'm very much in favour of celebrating a type of verse that often gets a raw deal from the highbrow contingent. I think it's important to demonstrate that funny poems are as valid and artistically serious as non-funny poems, and the best of this anthology provides strong evidence that this is the case. I'm not going to go through my favourite pieces in the book and attempt to say why they make me laugh, because there's nothing less conducive to humour than trying to analyse its every component, but I'll mention a few highlights which I hope will speak for themselves.

E. E. Cummings's 'Nobody Loses All the Time' is the story of Uncle Sol, a failed farmer who:

indulged in that possibly most inexcusable
of all to use a highfalootin phrase
luxuries that is or to
wit farming and be
it needlessly
added

my Uncle Sol's farm
failed because the chickens
ate the vegetables so
my Uncle Sol had a
chicken farm till the
skunks ate the chickens...

The catalogue of Uncle Sol's farming disappoint-ments continues until he eventually dies, is buried, and finally succeeds in starting a worm farm. It's E. E. Cummings's unique and addictive poetic voice that makes this poem so brilliant, and the speaker's self-awareness in those little asides such as "and be it needlessly added".

Auden's 'Give Me a Doctor' is another highlight:

Give me a doctor partridge-plump,
Short in the leg and broad in the rump,
An endomorph with gentle hands
Who'll never make absurd demands
That I abandon all my vices
Nor pull a long face in a crisis,
But with a twinkle in his eye
Will tell me that I have to die.

I love the idea of doctors behaving like this and, even more, the idea of a patient who actually wants his doctor to refer to his unavoidable death with "a twinkle in his eye".

Wendy Cope's 'Bloody Men' is also brilliant and, as with the Auden poem above, makes us laugh all the more because it is concerned with a real dilemma: the impossibility of making rational choices between two alternatives when you don't know what either will lead to:

Bloody men are like bloody buses.
You wait for about a year
And as soon as one approaches your stop
Two or three others appear...

If you make a mistake there is no turning back.
Jump off, and you'll stand there and gaze
While the cars and the taxis and lorries go by
And the minutes, the hours, the days.

Paul Durcan' s 'Tullynoe: Tête-à-tête in the Parish Priest's Parlour' is a hilarious dialogue poem which skilfully uses the aimless, repetitive quality of every-day conversation as a poetic form:

"Ah, he was a grand man."
"He was: he fell out of the train going to Sligo."
"He did: he thought he was going to the lavatory."
"He did: in fact he stepped out the rear door of the
train."
"He did: God, he must have got an awful fright."
"He did: he saw that it wasn't the lavatory at all.""...

On the darker side of the comic verse spectrum, there's Clive James's 'The Book of my Enemy has been Remaindered', a heart-warming revenge poem which I would strongly recommend to vindictive poetry enthusiasts:

The book of my enemy has been remaindered
And I rejoice.
It has gone with bowed head like a defeated legion
Beneath the yoke.
What avail him now his awards and prizes,
The praise expended upon his meticulous technique,
His individual new voice?
Knocked into the middle of next week...

Dorothy Parker's 'One Perfect Rose' is bitterly funny and questions the symbolism of love:

...Love long has taken for his amulet
One perfect rose.

Why is it no-one ever sent me yet
One perfect limousine, do you suppose?
Ah no, it's always just my luck to get
One perfect rose.

All the poems I've mentioned so far are excellent irrespective of their humour, and would deserve to be in any anthology. The less successful pieces included in this book are neither funny nor good poems; they come across as silly and pointless:

When Baby's cries grew hard to bear
I popped him in the Frigidaire
I never would have done so if
I'd known that he'd be frozen stiff.
My wife said: "George, I'm so *unhappé*
Our darling's now completely *frappé!*'
(*'L 'Enfant Glacé'* by Harry Graham)

The anthology contains a lot of very short poems, many of which are much better than this, like Roger McGough's 'Survivor':

> Everyday,
> I think about dying.
> About disease, starvation,
> violence, terrorism, war,
> the end of the world.
>
> It helps
> Keep my mind off things.

Is the speaker of the poem so selfish that the global misery he witnesses on the news actually cheers him up, because it's so much worse than his own problems, or is McGough trying to make the point that most people are less bothered about bad things in the abstract than the specific, niggly events that make their day-to-day lives more difficult?

I enjoyed discovering a few good poems I didn't previously know, and I think a lot of people will like this book. My main criticism of it is that there are too many things included which, although they contain a some funny moments, don't amount to much poetically.

SOPHIE HANNAH
IN WOKINGHAM ON BOXING DAY
AT THE EDINBURGH WOOLLEN MILL

Two earnest customers compare
a ribbed and unribbed sleeve.
I wonder what I'm doing here
and think I ought to leave,
get in my car and drive away.
  I stand beside the till
  in Wokingham on Boxing Day
  at The Edinburgh Woollen Mill.

All of the other shops are closed.
Most people are in bed.
Somehow I know that I'm supposed
to find an A-Z.
Somehow I sense I must obey
  an unfamiliar will
  in Wokingham on Boxing Day
  at The Edinburgh Woollen Mill.

I parked in a disabled space
so either I'm a cheat
or a debilitating case
of searching for your street
has started to erode away
  my locomotive skill
  in Wokingham on Boxing Day
  at The Edinburgh Woollen Mill,

somewhere perhaps you've never been.
I doubt you're into wool.
Even if mohair's not your scene
the atmosphere is full
of your proximity. I sway
    and feel a little ill
    in Wokingham on Boxing Day
    at The Edinburgh Woollen Mill.

The sales assistants wish me luck
and say they hope I find
the place I want. I have been stuck
with what I left behind,
with what I've been too scared to say,
    too scared to say until
    in Wokingham on Boxing Day
    at The Edinburgh Woollen Mill

I tell myself the time is now;
willingly I confess
my love for you to some poor cow
in an angora dress
whose get-lost-loony eyes convey
    her interest, which is nil,
    in Wokingham on Boxing Day
    at The Edinburgh Woollen Mill.

I find your house. You're still in bed.
I leave my gift and flee,
pleased with myself, not having said
how you can contact me,
driven by fears I can't allay,
    dreams I did not fulfil
    in Wokingham on Boxing Day
    at The Edinburgh Woollen Mill.

Chains are the most distressing shops.
They crop up everywhere.
Tbe point at which the likeness stops
squeezes my lungs of air.
When I see jumpers on display
    I wish that I was still
    in Wokingham on Boxing Day
    at The Edinburgh Woollen Mill.

ANN DRYSDALE
C*IT*S I*TER*UPT*S

Crosswords in bed. Last night we finished it
In the most satisfying way. Together.
Cries of discovery and of delight
As our thought-processes sparked one another
Made little echoes in our duvet-tent.
Clustered together round the anglepoise,
Signs of our cruciverbal element –
Two cocoas and a packet of rich teas.
Tonight was cheerless by comparison.
You called a sudden halt to the proceedings.
Said something hurtful, threw the crossword down
And turned your back to me and started reading.
A gust of wind slamming the gates of heaven;
A form of mental torture: 6, 11.

IAN SANSOM
SIGNS

L'enseigne fait la chalandise
La Fontaine

The sign in the doctor's says
"Do you know someone without a spleen?"

The sign outside the pub says
"Temporary Sign."

The sign in the butcher's says
"Pleased to Meet You, Meat to Please You."

The sign in the bookshop says
"Untranslated Literature."

The sign in the crematorium says
"No Smoking Beyond This Point."

The sign in the landlord's office says
"On Pregnancy Contracts Will Be Terminated."

ELIZABETH BARTLETT
DEAR BOY

Dear boy, I said, what you need
is a PLAN; sort out your priorities
if you can. I was Head of Department,
knew my way around; if you heed
what I say, who knows where you might
end up, a man like me perhaps.

There was nothing I didn't know about
freight and figures, even the commissionaire
wept when I left. I called him Bob
to show I wasn't a man to forget
that an ordinary man is just as rare
as me (to his wife, perhaps, or kids).
Look – er – Fred, I used to say, it's all
in the mind. Well, he was pathetic
really and in the executive bar we'd fall
about laughing at the way he stood there,
just opening and shutting the door
for us, the backbone of the company.

Dear boy, I said to the man I hired
to re-sand the parquet in the lounge,
I was Smith of the P.Q.R., you need
to watch what you say or you're fired.
He worked for himself it seemed.
I felt a bit odd that morning, newly retired,
but I know my stuff. Next day, early,
I took him on one side and said
I hadn't been serious about my warning,
that he could be head of a building firm
if he knew the right way to talk
and dress and learned how to play
golf. Turned out he was a Cambridge man,
liked using his hands he said, and May
balls and High Table were not for him.
He hadn't heard of the P.Q.R.
but he made a good job of the floor,
I'll say that for him, and when he left
I opened the door. Good-bye Laurence;
Larry, he said. Watching him go

I felt ill at ease and almost bereft.

For a few days I got a bit low,
scared the wife, moped around a bit,
but a few drinks did the trick.
Saw a chap on the dole in the pub, so
I said to him, Dear boy, I said,
what you need is a PLAN.
Took it the wrong way. I care,
I really care for people who don't
know about things the way I do,
and didn't expect to end up here,
but the young padre is a friend of mine,
though they say he's a queer,
so I said to him, Dear boy, dear boy,
I am alone and afraid, and what I need
is a PLAN, like any ageing dying man.
I really must have been below par,
I forgot to mention the P.Q.R.

JOHN HEGLEY
THE FAN

The man came up to me after the show
because he wanted me to know
that the poem about my dog being dead
had moved him.
"My own dog died yesterday
and what you wrote helped me out", he said.
"I'm not a poetry man
but that was O.K."
He told me how the expression of grief
for my own dog's curtains
had given him certain relief.
There were feelings which never quite came
            to the surface
after he'd dug his dog under the surface.
"It's just a shame", he added,
"that the one in your story
never had the same name as mine.
Perhaps you could change it for me.
Otherwise things might get a bit nasty".

PAUL GROVES

LIFE: MADE IN TAIWAN

Assemble. You will see the bits.
When they fit, baby will come after
though down the line. Keep it clean,
keep it warm; keep it refrigeration
of food. Watching it grow ever
and stronger son, or having daughter.
When it schooling make it violin:
this will be big bucks in adult showcase
with luckspin. Television with care.
Junk will be frowned. Our Company say
education: locksmith, animal clinic,
pearl high-tech with boats. Film,
as it (boy, girl) soon not young either
but American teenage type. Say
gum banned. Walking tall better.
Say about shoulders, and strong teeth.
We say fish because longevity.
All exam hardness good for bucks,
so our advice keen. Avoid horses.
Avoid old way, but gods good.
Wear glasses for clearer eyes.
Sport. American basketball. Dating
agency better than persons on corridor
or other floor. We say chromosomes
and blood test. Hard work mostly.
Components assembly and big toy.
Evenings saké and putting in laughter.
Courtship with cosmetic (Company
will advise askers: please ask).
Courtesy like parents. Virgin like parents
until multiplying marriage on Astroturf
with many thousand bride and groom.
Indoor climate and dome. No rain
on veil. We advise honeymoon night
only, with work prompt soon.
Assemble. You will see the bits.
When they fit, baby will come after
though down the line. Keep it clean,
keep it warm; keep it refrigeration.

Tenuous and Precarious: the Comic Muse

GWYNETH LEWIS ON THE ESCAPOLOGY OF VERSE

THE GROWTH IN the popularity of poetry slams has led some people to call poetry the new stand-up comedy. In a slam, I've noticed, some lowest-common-denominator humour is required to get you through the first round, while a victory in the second requires some degree of seriousness. There are, of course, superficial similarities between poems and jokes. Both require an unusually masochistic degree of self-revelation or, even, exhibitionism. A certain universality of subject matter is necessary for broad appeal. Topicality helps, but with reliance on older archetypes behind the occasion for satire. The joker must have an ear for common speech. Timing is everything.

Memory plays an important role in both crafts. Bob Monkhouse losing his joke book didn't stop him from performing virtuoso medleys of jokes, where the audience called out subjects as diverse as traffic, piles and the IMF for him to link together. Such memory takes preparation, fat notebooks behind the pause to think on stage. Notice how Ken Dodd uses his "Isn't it a lovely day for a ...." tag to gain time as he lines up the next jokes in his head. This is a real clue as to how the oral tradition worked – a set chorus would be most useful as you were racking your brain for what exactly the prince did say when he finally met the magic stag he'd been hunting.

I recently heard a story about a comedian who saw a younger man catastrophically die on stage. A year later they were on the same bill again and the young man couldn't say a word without making the audience crack up, even though his gags were exactly the same as before. The old comedian asked the younger after the show how on earth he'd turned his act around. He replied "I knew I had the material right but wasn't sure of the character". I recognise this as a thing that goes wrong with some poems. You can have all the pyrotechnics, images and descriptions you like lined up, but if the character speaking isn't sufficiently fully imagined, the poem will never convince. You need to know who is speaking, what their accent is and what kind of metrical shoes they wear on their feet.

I've been collecting jokes since I was a child. *Jack and Jill* used to have a riddles column but I didn't understand them all. This classic delighted me for

years – still does. Question: When is a door not a door? Answer: When it's ajar. The mystery was in the play on the indefinite article, and how it could become even more indefinite and disappear completely into the word "ajar". I still can't hear the word without seeing a jam jar with some water in it and, to go one step further into unconscious word play, a door jamb. The joke had taken me straight beyond frivolity into semantics, even though I didn't know it at the time.

An American cousin of mine told me an even more astonishing riddle recently, one which seems to me to capture the trick of poetry exactly. It goes like this: You're in a sealed room with nothing in it but a table and a mirror. How do you get out? The answer is: You look in the mirror, see what you saw. Take the saw, cut the table in half. Put the two into a whole. Escape through the hole. This kind of wit is an effort to loosen the buckles on the straight-jacket of ordinary thinking. It's a punning Houdini trick. You could argue that such a play on words is tautology but I'd say that the grappling with slightly different spellings of the same word gives you that little half-inch that can change your perspective and allow you to effect an escape from isolation into hilarity.

Stevie Smith knew that wit can be an expression not of levity but of its opposite:

> Tenuous and Precarious
> Were my guardians,
> Precarious and Tenuous,
> Two Romans.

Here she plays the portentousness of an important-sounding word against its meaning. In this case two weak people exercised a tyrannical power over the speaker – the play on words is amusing, but the message is tragic. This kind of wit is no laughing matter, it's an inoculation against despair. Such desperation leads to an Arabian Nights-like story-telling – anything to amuse, to keep people listening, to postpone the fact of you alone in a sealed room with no more puns to get you out.

Rhyme acts as a divining rod straight into our unconscious fears and obsessions. My sister and I used to like having *The Night Before Christmas* read to us as children. Our favourite part was the description of Santa Claus's "round little belly / That shook when he laughed / Like a bowl full of jelly". This used to make us hysterical. I think we were laughing at the ghost rhyme "willy", but part of the joke was that we weren't quite sure of Santa Claus's anatomy down there. Bathetic rhyming, often found in nonsense verse, is frequently an attempt to impose order on a chaotic world. One poem entitled 'Song' in Joseph Brodsky's last collection goes

> I wish you were here, dear,
> I wish you were here.
> I wish you sat on the sofa
> and I sat near.

These rhymes anxiously create an artistic proximity which the parted lovers don't enjoy in reality. The sound echoes are an effort of will and desire, but know themselves to be fragile.

Good jokes and poetry both allow us to think laterally about touchy subjects so that the mind can grasp solutions way out to the left of its normal field of vision. As the spate of Diana jokes has shown us this last year (and yes, I have a fine collection of those) comedy permits us to deal with painful subjects in a therapeutic way. The taboo needs to be broken, that blasphemy spoken. There's a Tom and Jerry cartoon which demonstrates this point neatly. The usual war between the two is set in Vienna. The cat notices that when there's waltz music playing the mouse can't stop himself dancing. So Tom learns to play the piano in order to lure his prey out of the mouse hole. The phenomenon of the cat-and-mouse double act becomes famous. While the music plays the two are friends. One sequence shows Tom playing the piano while Jerry waltzes with the cat's white-gloved paw as his partner. The minute the music stops the two are mortal enemies again. For me this captures how poetry and pain work in tandem: while the music plays they find a way of being together in safety. Stop the beat, though, and they're at each other's throats. Miserable poets don't make better art, but writing can have a therapeutic effect on neurosis if we're given the safety of rhythm, metre and rhyme to pacify the potentially destructive side-effects of introspection. Far from being an optional extra, poetic form – or the threefold structure of a potentially upsetting joke – has a homeopathic effect on pain, makes it safe for us to look at a subject which might, otherwise, be too much for us to bear. One

of the more tasteless Diana jokes in my little book (which I won't quote here) involved a second-rate genie whose lamp has been rubbed by Prince Charles. He's unable to grant the Prince's first request but he thinks he can grant the second. I was astonished to look back and find exactly the same comic device used in a Gulf War joke in 1991 when the ITV regional franchises were being auctioned off by the government. In that gag the genie is asked to do something about Saddam Hussein. He plays for time and begs his lord and master to make an easier request. "What about letting HTV (the Welsh ITV company) retain their franchise?". "OK", says the genie "Let's have a go at Saddam Hussein!"

Of course, fixed forms such as sonnets, villanelles and sestinas do have certain folds of thought in them, acting as a mnemonic structure. Compared to prose, poetry is easy to memorise, especially if it rhymes. Jokes are notoriously difficult to remember. The trick is to recall the structure, rather than the punchline. If you don't set up the gag correctly you'll end up fumbling, saying "Wait a minute, just let me get this right" and boring all your friends. Indeed, rhyme is a poem's punchline, but it mustn't be its main *raison d'être*. Let me quote a *Two Ronnies* sketch. Ronnie Corbett comes into an ice cream parlour wearing a motorcycle helmet. You wonder about the helmet and want to see what has to happen to make it part of the sketch. He asks for some salt-and-vinegar-flavoured ice cream. Ronnie Barker says he doesn't have any but reels off a virtuoso list of sweet flavours. "What, not even cheese and onion?" retorts Corbett. Barker rattles off another long list including tutti frutti, fruits of the forest, butterscotch, apricot, and so forth. At the end of this performance Corbett announces confidently "I'll take smoky bacon". Whereupon Barker hits him on the head with a frying pan. You have to see it…. but the helmet is the rhyme of the joke, the point to which the whole gag is pushing, its punchline. It's not, however, the main substance of the comedy, which is the play on the idea of savoury ice cream. The couplet at the end of a sonnet is a reader's destination, but the journey is in the movement of the octave and the sestet.

One important technique common both to jokes and many poems is what I call the Give the Dog a Bone trick. It consists of tying up the listener's attention with a complete red herring, only to bring in a totally unexpected solution when the mind's barriers are down and therefore unable to resist it. The mind's guard dog eats the drugged meat, falls asleep and let the burglars in to snaffle the video. Here are two quick examples. A pig goes into a Job Centre wanting work. The lady behind the counter says "I've got just the job for you" and sends him off for an interview. Next day he's back. "What's wrong?" "You sent me to a circus. That's no good to me. I'm a plumber". Here what's questioned is our assumption that animals don't have qualifications. In the next joke it's our lumping of animals together in one group that's challenged. Two horses are talking in a pub about having their balls squeezed at the start of their recent races. A dog calls in, says that the same thing happened to him. "Did you hear that?", says one of the horses, astonished, "A talking dog!". Poems use this technique of distraction all the time to smuggle the real story into the wary viewer's mind before they are ready to defend themselves against it. A prime example of this kind of poem is *Paradise Lost.* The epic seems to be entirely about Adam and Eve and the Fall but large sections describing the rebel angels are, in fact, about the politics of the Civil War.

I've concentrated so far on some similarities of techniques used between jokes and poems. There is, however, a philosophical extension to this argument. Auden said that Christ's crucifixion had abolished the distinction between comedy and tragedy. I've always been haunted by the epilogue of Chaucer's *Troilus and Criseyde* where, following the lovers' trials and tribulations Troilus looks down on the world and laughs at their joint misfortunes:

> And in hymself he lough right at the wo
> Of hem that wepten for his deth so faste:
> And dampned al oure werk that foloweth so
> The blynde lust, the which that may not laste,
> And sholden al oure herte on heven caste.
> And forth he wente, shortly for to telle,
> Ther as Mercurye sorted hym to dwelle.

It's a miraculous hilarity, free of attachment and ego, a life-giving perspective which doesn't diminish pain but shifts the terms so that we can, at least for a moment, be free of it. It's Mother Theresa getting to the Pearly Gates and being granted a wish by St. Peter. Would she like to save the poor? No. Cure the sick? No, she says firmly. "I want to direct".

GEE WILLIAMS
CAN'T COOK, DON'T COOK

not just alone but without you
nothing would be diced spiced sliced iced
not even a cockle sacrificed,
no not once, let alone twice or thrice

hardly an ingredient would be
boiled broiled oiled and foiled
then from reading Our Mutual Friend
that bit too long allowed to spoil

on that cruel steel rack a space
where now under the grill brill and dill
linger and dream of the moist bed of lentil
that I steeped simmered contrived to spill.

JANE HOLLAND
A MEMO TO MALE POETS

You always write from someone else's
point of view. You use short words.
You alternate with longer ones.
                                    You are clever,
very clever. You have letters after your name,
an entire alphabet of understanding.

You wield rude words with the half-daring,
half-insouciant air of a schoolboy
chucking conkers at a car.

They make no impact. They bounce back
off the windscreen of poetry like sky,
nothing but light, reflection.

You talk of soccer and politics
as if they were one and the same,
which maybe they are. I can't be sure.

You drag your sorry love-affairs
into anthologies, and don't apologize.

It's art, and art is what it is.

You give us your respect and half a page
in all-inclusive summaries. You throw big names
like Adcock into space
                            (and hope their sling-shot orbit
gives you all a well-earned rest).

But watch your backs, we're creeping up on you.

We've torn that locker poster down.
We've put our feet up on the furniture.
You are no longer safe. Sucks boo.

And if we choose to screw a few of you,
don't think that means it's all okay,
we've knuckled under once again.

We're simply doing what you do,
only rather better.

JOHN MOLE
THE MOBILE RAG

Out of your pocket, up to your face,
Any occasion, any old place,
Dial those digits, watch this space
Doing the mobile,
It's in the bag,
Yes, doing the mobile rag.

Chase your client, hurry that lunch,
Bend your ear, let your shoulder hunch,
Hear those Japanese numbers crunch
Doing the mobile,
Porsch or Jag,
Yes, doing the mobile rag.

Stride down the platform, turn on your heel,
Swagger and strut from deal to deal,
Small cogs know that you're the big wheel
Doing the mobile
Light up a fag,
Yes, doing the mobile rag.

Put in the boot, sharpen the knife,
This is the action, this is the life,
Always cut short the call from your wife
Doing the mobile,
Nag nag nag,
Doing the mobile rag.

Honour your partner? Keep your old car?
Who the hell do they think you are!
Look at that split skirt over by the bar
Doing the mobile,
Good for a shag,
Doing the mobile rag.

Wire up the e-mail, tighten the net,
Shaft your department without regret,
There's room at the top and you'll make it yet
Doing the mobile,
Doing the mobile,
Doing that mobile rag.

Why Funny Poems Never Win National Poetry Competitions

A QUESTIONNAIRE BY JOHN WHITWORTH

1. Matthew Arnold said Pope and Dryden were monuments of our prose not our poetry. Has this remark any bearing on poetry's dearth of jokes?

2. In the genre (which I have just invented) of the seaside poem which do you prefer - 'Dover Beach' or 'The Walrus And The Carpenter?' Which is the more important? Can Light Verse be important? Is importance important?

3. Funny Poets are often *Daily Telegraph* readers. I am. Is this not absolutely fatal?

4. Dr Johnson preferred Shakespeare's comedies to his tragedies. What is he on about? Can the man be serious?

5. Sullivan felt Gilbert dragged him down. Without Gilbert he wrote *The Lost Chord* and a very long and boring opera called *Ivanhoe*. He did, however, get his knight hood first. Is there a moral in this?

6. You are a judge in the National Poetry competition? You want to give first prize to a funny poem about babies. Do you think you are going to get away with it?

7. I think Ogden Nash is funny? Kingsley Amis doesn't think Ogden Nash is funny. Which is right?

8. Jeffrey Archer may become the Mayor Of London. How can you make jokes at a time like this?

9. You are about to read your poems at A Poetry Reading. Which of these voices would you adopt?

    a. The Olivier Richard III staccato (men only)
    b. The Downmarket Regional Incomprehensible
    c. The Dark Mutter (alternatively The Dark Nutter)
    d. The Head Prefect E–L–O–C–U–T–I–O– N–A– R–Y (women only)

10. Which of these is a True Poet?

    a.   The Priest/Bard
    b.   The Unacknowledged Legislator Of Mankind
    c.   The Egg Head
    d.   The Clown who farts 'Jerusalem'

11. Two XIs for the Poetry Olympics.

Non-Jokers	Jokers
Ted Spenser	Geoff Chaucer
Big Bill Wordsworth	Jackie Dryden
'Byssh-o' Shelley	Rabbit Burns
Emmie Bronte	'Lord George' Byron
Matt Arnold	Wystie Auden
Willy Yeats	Stevie Smith
Long Tom Eliot	Little John Betjeman
Hard Hughie MacDiarmid	Bigfoot Larkin
Geoff Hill	Gav Ewart
Sylv Plath	Wend Cope
Ted Hughes	Kit Wright

Billy Shakespeare (referee)

THREE POEMS BY KIT WRIGHT
A LIGHT TOAST

Hurray, its Air Commodore Nigel Vance
with his Lo Fat Paprika Substitute,
containing up to 50 per cent less fat
than regular paprika!
"*Tiens*", writes Mrs Feast of Snape,
I can hardly believe it isn't the genuine thing!"

"I've got into trousers", writes an excited
half-fat Colonel Wotherspoon,
"I haven't been able to wear since before the war.
What's more, I'm enjoying my goulash more than ever –
and eating twice as much of it!"

Nice one, Air Commodore!
I raise to the sky
my glass of semi-skimmed whisky
as you skim by.

CLASSICAL VS ROMANTIC

Jane Austen
Kept her legs crausten
Contrast to Emily Brontë
Who displayed the Full Montë.

AL CAPONE

Al Capone
Grew the worst cabbages known.
Disgusted with brassica,
He organised the St Valentine's Day Massacre.

JOHN FULLER
QUICKER BY THE KLEINE

At Grindelwald one Frederick Fletcher
Desired me to inscribe his *Manfred.*
He cried: "My Lord, I shall be candid.
A grocer cannot understand it".
I stuck my stock into the gletscher
And told him kindly: "No one *can,* Fred.
You have to read it with persistence.
Ideally you should read left-handed,
And when you feel you're *in der Quetsche*
Look to your sister for assistance".

Under the duvet Nanny's calling,
Promising a sticky kiss;
The Lorelei is crooning in
Her bottomless crevasse of bliss;
Here on the Jungfrau snow is falling
With a delicious sense of sin.
Manfred drives a grocer frantic
Insisting that he's not romantic
(Romanticism is enthralling;
A grocer's everything that's Swiss).

Hell is the grandest of hotels.
Hell is gemütlich and quite roomy
(I have one foot already there).
I make a thing of being gloomy
But don't particularly care.
Drown me in the Dardanelles!
Hang me, and so despatch me neck first!
Blacken my actions in the *Chronicle!*
I'll simply smile, adjust my monocle
And mock the headline over breakfast.

I limp the high exclusive line
Which cannot take account of grocers
Even my breakfast is a grossness
That I can scarce acknowledge mine.
I am ascetic in moroseness:
I actually enjoy the guilt
Poetically, without neurosis.

It's just the way my psyche's built.
It's like the bubbles in my wine.
It's like the swagger in my kilt.

Let grocers cross the Grosse Scheidegg!
I shall do something altogether
More appropriate to the weather
And modulate into the minor.
Sing me to sleep beneath the eaves!
Spring will come, with fresher leaves
(Spoonfuls of leaves, in fact, a quarter
Of lemon and some boiling water).
I'll break my fast on tea not fried egg
And get there quicker by the Kleine.

Simon Rae on English Humour

WHERE, THE LATE and much-missed Willie Rushton was wont to inquire, would we be without humour? before, with impeccable timing, supplying the answer: Germany. I am far too ignorant to know whether the great German poets can be charged with humourlessness. For all I know, Schiller had them rolling in the aisles, bierkellers resounded with raucous laughter at the latest irresistible squib from Goethe, and Heine was a stand-up comic before taking to his chaise longue for good; but my brief acquaintance with Carlyle, than whom no one was more steeped in German literature, suggests otherwise.

By contrast, English poetry is full of humour. From Chaucer to Cope, with the exception of a tedious old bore like Wordsworth – that's unfair: he was a tedious young bore as well – English poets have been instinctively prone to comedy. Even a depressive like Cowper was capable of producing a naturally funny poem on occasion, and all the truly great poets (Milton is a special case – though there is a rather donnish joke somewhere in *Paradise Lost*), have genuinely funny work somewhere in the canon. This remains true of the twentieth century: Auden, Lawrence, Larkin, Hughes, Stevie Smith, Betjeman were all serious poets who could be seriously funny. Even T. S. Eliot, though he made it clear that he was condescending to leave the dais of high art to do so, took a turn at being amusing. And the tradition continues quite healthily to this day – Raine, Reid, Fenton, Armitage, Maxwell, McMillan, Whitworth, Sophie Hannah...

Humour is such a constant in English poetry as to be hardly worth remarking. Books could, and perhaps should he written to explain it, but for poets and readers alike, it appears to be simply one of those glorious givens, like the English weather. Where indeed would we be without it?

TWO POEMS BY ALISON PRYDE
SAVE PAPER: RECYCLE A POEM

Old sailor, village bore,
Catches guest at church door.
Leaves him feeling very cross,
Blames that bloody albatross.

Walked a lot for hours and hours,
Saw some pretty yellow flowers.
Didn't know names of the hills,
But think the flowers were daffodils.

Our pest controller uses a pipe,
He's good, no corpses and no smell
And for a Deutschmark extra,
He'll sort the kids as well.

English villagers are a lovesome lot,
Though some can be a bit funny.
Why don't you wind that old church clock?
And bugger me, that's the same jar of honey.

Bird sings, quite good.
Goes further into wood.
Feel depressive, quite excessive.
Knew I should.

"I've been called a lot of things, but never a sacred river",
Mused Alph. "What a funny notion".
"Oh, I don't know", said his friend Fred, "When you've had
A potion, down at the Damsel and Dulcimer,
You don't 'alf meander with a mazy motion".

Wish I was back
For the start of the tax year.
I say this, sitting prettily
In Italy.

Thus Satan to his angel cohorts spake:
        "Where the hell is it?"

Sir Lancelot
Felt such a clot,
Singing, "Tirra lirra".
The Lady of Shalott
Cared not a jot.
She was bothered about that mirror

ON TRYING TO FIND "HAPPY" POEMS

Poets are a gloomy lot,
God wot,
ink blot,
A happy life with loving wife and cheery tot,
a country cott
in rustic spot
with garden plot
are what
it's not.
No, doom and gloom are what
we've got
Greasy Joan doth keel the pot,
the snot-
-ful tot
whinges a lot.
The garden plot
has black spot,
the country cott
has dry rot
and wet rot.
the upshot
is: our poor poet, the dull clot,
the crackpot,
legs it off at a brisk trot
to become a drunken sot,
and who is there who cares a jot?
Life's not
so hot,
God wot.
poets are a gloomy lot.

Think Three Times: You're Joking

by Siân Hughes

ROGER McGOUGH

The Spotted Unicorn: The Diaries of Chi Wen Tzu

Penguin, £8.99
ISBN 0 670 87974 6

ALFRED BRENDEL

One Finger Too Many

Faber, £7.99
ISBN 0 571 19618 7

Chi Wen Tzu always thought three times before taking action. Twice would have been quite enough.

THIS CONFUCIAN PEARL leads Roger McGough to wonder "what manner of man always reflected thrice before acting?" Someone "indecisive", "inventive" and "brilliant" – a joke-teller, in fact, an artist, a stretcher of logic, someone who can be relied on to take things at least one step too far. *The Spotted Unicorn* can be said to be built entirely on this one joke except that the joke itself seems to be about the nature of all joking: after all – think once, you exist, think twice, you're wise, think three times, you're joking! Like all the best jokes it relies to some extent on echoes of other codes, on a conversational to-ing and fro-ing that exaggerates, diverts, and refers back on itself.

A winning tactic of the master joke-teller is an ability to slip into another voice. Mock-translation is a well-established mode for poetry – one more usually reserved for revealing dark secrets or political dissent than for using silly voices – but all the more ingenious here for avoiding any sense of an irritating darker significance.

Because it would spoil it to start in the middle, this is the diarist's first entry:

Tonight, young wife lying naked
on panda-skin rug. Full moon

hanging in sky like Chinese lampshade
(one of those round white ones).

Having chosen the third and least promising of three possible responses to this sight –

Open bottle of rice-wine,
write up day's events in diary,
relax in warm bath, then make love?

– the diarist opens the following day with news that "young wife" has left for her mother's – "Not like being woken up at 4a.m. / by drunken diarist". The absence of young wife leaves him in some dilemma about supper. Takeaway? Hard Wok Cafe? or "Crack open third bottle of rice-wine / and see how feel later?" No contest, really. This proves what all fairy-tales know – third options are for those who wish to go beyond existence and wisdom into the realms of drink, poetry, chance, and dinner-service design.

My only moment of regret in reading the anti-wisdom of Chi Wen Tzu was that I had read enough of the blurb to spoil a few of its surprises, so I hesitate before letting my natural enthusiasm give away too many of them here: his response to New Generation Chinese Poetry, the invention of haiku, his prefiguring some of the best-loved works of English literature ("Sing of dappled things! / Freckled legs and picked eggs / Budgies' wings. Nipples."), the original irritation caused by chopsticks on the piano, the acupuncture repair outfit, and of course how the unicorn came to be spotted.

Satoshi Kitamura's drawings delight in the same kind of detail that will bring readers back over and over to the text – look out for a perplexed duck that keeps reappearing, the mouse on the poet's computer, the modern-art version of a landscape in his study, alphabetti braid on his kimono and unexpected party debris.

I've heard comic poetry in general, and Roger McGough's work in particular, defended for its democratic qualities, for the fact that non-poetry lovers can be taken along for a good night out, and non-poetry-readers bought a book of the stuff they won't hate, on the basis that this might lead them on to "better", more serious reading – hand them a joint today, and they'll buy heroin from you tomorrow. Yes, this finely-poised piece of whimsy would delight the most accidental viewer of the latest Nation's Favourite programme, its in-jokes make you laugh rather than making you feel clever, but it would be good to abandon the "conversion-rate" approach to the work of poetry's most popular ambassador – after all, an addict is an addict, and you can pass me this joint as often as you like, it's good stuff.

Alfred Brendel

In their different ways Roger McGough's *The Spotted Unicorn* and Alfred Brendel's *One Finger Too Many* are literary curiosities – slim, witty, restrained, and collectable – but where Roger McGough's slim volume is collectable as much as a set of words to repeat, play with, read aloud and mis-quote in the bath, Brendel's is collectable primarily as an artefact. His supernatural zoo, both animal and human, has more to it than mere charm, and the recur-rent chickens in themselves were enough to hold my interest, but the poems (originally written in German; English versions by the author with Richard Stokes) rested more snugly on the page than in my mouth, and I'd be surprised to find myself learning any by heart. It's hard not to look for music in poems by a famous musician, and not to see their status as translations as a kind of score.

In the postscript, the poet says "There are, among my muses, a number of old ladies". His other muses are Brahms, and the animals of his "depraved imagination". The best moments are those that approach most nearly either the bizarre worlds of the old ladies or a kind of detached depravity, or better still, a combination of both –

When the old lady
first took the chicken to bed with her
she didn't give it a second thought

It was chilly outside and the chicken
friendly by nature
slipped between the sheets

Actually

the old lady resembled a chicken
Like many chickens
she failed to finish sentences
shuffled her feet and brooded

Trading on the sparse, tentative quality of trans-lation, Brendel is most successful at moments of prosaic lightness – a deliberate skirting away from telling the story – but occasionally his telling on past the end of the joke becomes less rather than more funny. 'Sultan' the story of a man with a wife "and seventeen stand-ins" whose life "wasn't so bad after all" despite the prob-lems he had telling them apart, concludes adeptly with:

When
in addition
they showed talent
he could be relied upon
and the palace kitchen was
renowned

But the finger of the title poem had one adventure too many for me – I wanted it to stop at the moment when everyone is perplexed by his knocking on the pianist's head during a concert:

Whatever it wished to denounce
remained a mystery
for clearly the pianist was doing his best
and the audience
at such moments
held its breath

Call me difficult to please, but I'm always a bit disappointed when poems about chickens and ghosts and camels and dead composers turn out to be really about chickens, ghosts, camels and dead composers – or was I missing something? Perhaps the extra finger of the title effectively labels all the apparitions, opposites and alternative endings of this collection as extras, asides, impossibilities, mischief. I won't knock my head too hard with my mischief finger in response. After all, the pianist was doing his best, and the audience, at such moments, is enjoying itself well enough...

ROGER MCGOUGH
THE WRITTEN WORD
(A Full Monty of Poetic Forms)

A poet of little repute
        Desperate for something to do
One evening pissed as a newt
        Decided to have a tattoo.

On his chest an unrhymed sestina
        On his belly a fine villanelle
On each bicep a series of haiku
        On each shank a tanka as well.

On each shoulder a petrarchan sonnet
        Making twenty-eight lines in all
An acrostic across each firm buttock
        With a limerick, what else? on each ball.

On each knee, though knobbly, a rondeau redoublé
        (which was terribly tricky to do)
On each pendulous lobe, a pindaric ode
        On each clavicle, a neat clerihew.

Any flesh that remained was minutely quatrained
        (the odd couplet if not enough room)
On the sole of each foot, a virelai was put
        An englyn and Malaysian pantoum.

* * *

This poet of Great Repute
        Now travels from town to town
Goes on stage, removes his shirt
        And takes his trousers down

While audiences marvel
        At the body of work so vast
Concrete, surreal and post-modern
        Alongside the great works of the past.

And some are poetry-lovers
    Who believe they could do worse
Than curl up every evening
    With this anthology of verse.

For nothing can beat the written word
Especially on a torso, bared.

VERNON SCANNELL
GOOD TIME

How that ravenous abstraction, Time,
can own the quality of goodness, goodness
knows; and yet we say it all the time.

Have a good time is simple, I suppose;
at least we catch the drift: enjoy yourself,
get drunk, get laid, get tanned, or all of those.

Joy buds and flowers in Time, that's understood;
that which is indispensable to bliss,
its soil and habitation, must be good.

But when they say, as they quite often do,
all in good time, what can be meant by this?
I've usd the phrase myself, and so have you.

No one, though, has ever told as why
the time is "good" that everything is in:
I can't explain, however hard I try.

Language games are always hit or miss;
you might not learn much but they can be fun.
In fact I had a good time writing this.

SIMON RAE

THE PENIS IN THE FIELD (A COMPANION PIECE)

When the farmer, taking a shortcut home,
comes across it will he know what it is?
Will he pick it up in a hanky
and accelerate to the police?
             (Matthew Sweeney, 'In A Field')

I was the farmer, and it was in my field.
I knew exactly what it was,
though I was surprised to see it
just there by the kissing-gate;
the kissing-gate you can in fact
just see from the combine's cabin
as you turn at the top of the nine acre.

And I did wrap it up in my handkerchief.
But not to show the police.
No, what formal identification there was
took place at home, on the kitchen table,
before I threw it into the pail for the pigs

and slammed the door on the screaming
to check that the knife at least,
with its nicked blade and string-bound handle,
was still where I'd put it – six inches
under the dirt under the hen-coop.

RICHARD BRISTOWE

MAN IN BLACK BLUES

Over the terrace the wet wind blows,
There's ice in my hair and a cold in my nose.

The coins come shimmering out of the sky,
I'm a League referee, I don't know why.

A tackle, a dive: which is worse?
Each comes wrapped in a four-letter curse.

A wet yellow card, names in the book,
Ali would be proud of that last left hook.

The spit comes spattering out of the sky,
I'm a League referee, I don't know why.

I run to the spot; free kick, indirect:
Off to the left there are seats being wrecked.

They scream that I haven't got eyes in my head,
They howl that my parents have never been wed.

Will I ever get home, will I get to my car?
The pain throbs deep in my hernia scar.

There's mud in my whistle and spit in my eye,
I'm a League referee, I don't know why.

ROBERT SAXTON
THE SHAMBLES

Street names flash blood mischief past your censor.
Beneath the cobbles retch the ghosts of slaughter.
Taxis ply the outskirts, will ride no deeper.
Shambolic dogs nose back towards the Plaza

(Smarts of teargas, hops of drunken sailor),
Lope round a drunken corner: lo! Copacabana.
I ask about that girl from *Panorama,*
And all you hear's no cowboy's even seen her,

Not since the night she gambled with the shaman
And lost the lot: the flat, the cat, her savings.
One asks, then in a moment all's forgotten,

Her spirit-flight one-way like notes to Santa,
Letters of searchlight love franked Ipanema,
Spangled with sand shadowless dreams wear down to.

SARAH WARDLE
HUBRIS

I am a white man.
It is my goal to bring
my gods, my laws, my fighting
into your country, to penetrate upstream
as far as I can.
I have a dream.

I have a dream
to expand my mill,
to found a hospital for the ill.
My workers' health will benefit.
I have a scheme
and I shall profit.

And I shall profit
from the Judgement of Christ.
For I am good. I proselytize.
I speak in tongues to convert the heathen.
If I talk enough of it,
I shall go to heaven.

I shall go to heaven
with *you,* my dear.
With your big, blue eyes and your long, blonde hair
I can be sure that you will breed
a race of men
to carry on my greed.

TWO POEMS BY DUNCAN FORBES
EQUAL OPPORTUNISM

My personal computer is politically correct:
It agrees with E. M. Forster that if only we connect
The world would be much better for electors and elect.
It's been to universities and as you might expect
Has honorary doctorates and dozens to collect.
It's party apolitical and wholly circumspect:
With a reading age of 50 and a Mensa intellect,
It scans the Sunday papers and it never could neglect
The poor of any country – it can e-mail them direct.
Where bigotry's obligatory, it's certain to reject
The sexist or sectarian of either sex or sect.
With its unbiased judgement it would never deselect
The redhead or the dreadlocked, the freckled or the flecked.
Its spelling is as spelling goes impeccably well checked,
So clean in thought and verbiage it could never interject
A blasphemous excretive or words to that effect.
It's read the works of Kipling and *Collected Plays* of Brecht
And when it speaks in German, the Deutsch is ultra *echt.*
It doesn't smoke, it never drinks, nor fornicates erect.
It wears no prophylactics having nothing to protect,
No intravenous penis and nothing to inject.
It's not a phallic symbol and no hen has ever pecked
Its status or equipment which you're welcome to inspect:
It's taken twenty centuries to patent and perfect.
It's genuinely neuter and one of the select,
Both confidant(e) and tutor, though as it may suspect,
Because my libidego has a chauvinist effect,
My personal correctness is politically wrecked.

BEST BEFORE END

dot dot dot the future
stop full stop the past
there's no dot like the present
and dash it will not last.

BRIAN FEWSTER
THE COMMITTEE

There's one in nursery teaching
And one in holy orders,
And others have the silhouettes
Of police or prison warders.

It isn't hard to eavesdrop
Upon their conversation,
Where measured praise is condiment
To overall damnation.

With never-failing patience,
They sit in constant session.
The power of absolution
Is not in their possession.

They take my deposition
Concerning each depravity
Through microphones implanted
Inside the cranial cavity.

At night they're hyperactive,
With polymorphic faces,
To rubberneck and nose about
The dark secluded places.

Negotiating keyholes
As easily as vapour,
They crawl through my unconsciousness
Like sparks on smouldering paper,

And while my sleeping system
Flies blind on automatic,
Directions lost for routes I've crossed
Still crackle through the static.

THE CLASSIC POEM

SELECTED BY CAROLE SATYAMURTI

THIS IS NOT the first well-loved poem to be loved for the wrong reasons. Like Housman's, Frost's complexity can be concealed behind simplicity. I recently did a straw poll – what did people think 'The Road Not Taken' is saying? I did this because, until I learned it by heart, I had myself misunderstood it. Answers: that it celebrates the courage of choosing not to follow the crowd; that a choice made at a crucial point can shape the rest of one's life.

But the poem is a subtle meditation on the myths we live by, and calls into question the meaningfulness of choice itself. It expresses pessimism both about whether our much agonized-over choices are consequential at all, and about our ability to face the fact that they are not. And beyond personal myth-making, perhaps the poem is gently de-bunking the American myth of a self-made society based on purposeful choice.

It's a thoroughly modern, even post-modern, poem – meaning is what we make it, life is (nothing but?) the stories we tell about it.

Wonderfully, the language and the tone of the poem seduce the reader into precisely the kind of delusion (the misreading) that the speaker predicts for himself – or at least for his listeners.

ROBERT FROST
THE ROAD NOT TAKEN

Two roads diverged in a yellow wood,
And sorry I could not travel both
And be one traveller, long I stood
And looked down one as far as I could
To where it bent in the undergrowth;

Then took the other, as just as fair,
And having perhaps the better claim,
Because it was grassy and wanted wear;
Though as for that the passing there
Had worn them really about the same,

And both that morning equally lay
In leaves no step had trodden black.
Oh, I kept the first for another day!
Yet knowing how way leads on to way,
I doubted if I should ever come back.

I shall he telling this with a sigh
Somewhere ages and ages hence:
Two roads diverged in a wood, and I –
I took the one less travelled by,
And that has made all the difference.

Reprinted by permission of Jonathan Cape Ltd from Robert Frost, *Collected Poems*.

A SECOND LOOK

"A Black Giant"

ELAINE FEINSTEIN ON THE LEGACY OF PUSHKIN

ALEXANDER SERGEEVICH PUSHKIN (1799-1837) is, without contest, Russia's greatest poet. Yet in the West his work is chiefly known through opera; Mussorgsky's *Boris Godunov* for instance, or Tchaikovsky's *Evgeny Onegin* and *Queen of Spades.* Why should that be?

The most obvious answer is that the clarity and simplicity of Pushkin's language have made him peculiarly resistant to translation. The poetry of striking metaphors always translates easily; Pushkin often writes without imagery of any kind, relying on effortless, colloquial vigour and an extraordinary felicity of form which is hard to capture in English. The Russian language has a case structure which enables his meaning to remain clear whatever the order of his words, while English is uncomfortable with the least distortion of word order to achieve rhyme. Without his shapeliness, Pushkin's miraculous lucidity can sound pretty flat in English. But if that is the case, what is there to make Pushkin of interest to someone who loves poetry, but cannot read him in Russian?

To begin with, the man himself is an intriguing and paradoxical figure. He was the child of a feckless Russian aristocrat and a descendant of the African slave who became a favourite of Peter the Great. He lived under an autocracy more tyrannical than any other in Europe; his poems in praise of personal freedom aroused the suspicion of two tsars, and were found among the papers of all the leading figures in the Decembrist revolt (1825). He was not, however, taken into the confidence of the conspirators, who distrusted his reckless ebullience.

Pushkin had affairs with some of the most beautiful women of his time, and once wrote a Don Juan list of their first names into the album of a young girl; nevertheless, he always believed himself ugly, perhaps because his mother, herself known as the "beautiful creole", mocked him so cruelly in his childhood. Pushkin's own sketches often exaggerate his African appearance. It was an inheritance in which he took great pride, though in a poem 'To Yurev', written in 1820, he impudently made fun of his descent as a sexual disability:

'Pushkin and Onegin'. Sketch by Pushkin, 1824.

> While I, always an idle rake
> Ugly descendant of a Black
> Reared in a wilderness, can take
> No pleasure in the pains of
> love.
> Whenever I have won a beauty
> It is through shameless, hot
> desire
> That leads a nymph, still innocent
> To flush in an embarassment
> She does not fully understand
> And stealthily observe a satyr.

Many of his loveliest lyrics are about the pain of being abandoned or the torments of jealousy, and they are written as directly as if he were thinking aloud:

> How can you receive him in the reckless
> Hours before morning, half dressed,
> Without your mother or companion?
> I am loved, aren't I? You are so tender

When we are alone, your kisses are like fire.
Beloved friend, please give up this torture.
You don't know how very much I love you
You don't know how thoroughly I suffer.

When Pushkin decided to marry, he chose for his wife the beautiful seventeen-year-old Natalya Goncharova, some thirteen years younger than himself, who loved balls and clothes and took little interest in literature. She attracted the attentions of a handsome French officer, Baron d'Anthes, and at 37, Pushkin was killed in a duel fought to defend her honour; his early death was as poignant a waste as Mozart's.

All the Russian writers Western readers love have recorded their debts to Pushkin, including prose writers such as Gogol – to whom Pushkin, with prodigal generosity, gave the plots of *Dead Souls* and the *Inspector General* – and Tolstoy, Turgenev, and Dostoevsky. For my part, it was the enthusiasm of Marina Tsvetaeva and Anna Akhmatova that led me to my own vision of Pushkin.

Pushkin by Egor Geitman and sketches by Pushkin.

Tsvetayeva portrays the poet as quintessentially an outsider. She remembered how, when she visited the Pushkin monument in Moscow as a child, the blackness of the stone seemed a revelation: "A black giant among white children... The Russian poet... is a *Negro*". The apparent cause of the duel, Natalya Goncharova, was an unimportant factor in her idiosyncratic version of Pushkin's tragedy. All Russian poets, she insisted, were visibly different from, and inevitably cast out or struck down by, the conformist multitude. Tsvetaeva herself fell in love with Pushkin's poetry at the age of six, drawn to that remarkable moment of female exposure at the climax of *Evgeny Onegin* when Tatyana rejects her lover in the name of marital duty and declares: "I love you. Why pretend?". Tatyana has a candour which becomes the touchstone for all Tsvetaeva's own frankness.

Perhaps *Evgeny Onegin* is where an English reader should begin. The outline of the story is quickly told, and if it seems slight, so might the plot of a Jane Austen novel without the commenting voice of the author. *Evgeny Onegin* goes to live in the country, and there makes friends with Lensky, a young poet engaged to marry a neighbour's daughter, Olga Larina. Mainly out of boredom, Onegin agrees to visit the Larin household and Olga's elder sister, Tatyana, falls in love with him. Being altogether without coquetry, Tatyana writes a letter declaring her love, which Onegin refuses, on the grounds that he could make no woman a faithul husband. At Tatyana's name-day party, Onegin amuses himself by flirting with Lensky's Olga, and this leads to a duel in which Onegin kills his friend. After some years of guilty wandering, Onegin returns to St Petersburg to find Tatyana has married a wealthy and powerful Prince, and become a beauty. He pursues her eagerly, but she takes no notice of him. At length, he finds her weeping over one of his letters, but she still rejects him, with that poignant honesty Tsvetaeva so much admired.

In what sense is this a great *poem* for those who cannot enjoy the intoxication of the Onegin stanza Pushkin invented and handles so deftly? Pushkin writes as if he had heard Pound's advice that poetry should be at least as well-written as good prose. There are no epic images or long descriptions. Yet as Pushkin details his hero's dissipated life of pleasure in the capital, he brings the whole of St Petersburg to life around the reader: the restaurants, the theatre rustling and glittering before a ballet, weary coachmen asleep in their furs while their masters dance, a pretty girl on her morning milk round. And, in case you think these excitements are only for those who read Russian, there are at least two translations, which give a sense of Pushkin's laconic vividness. (James E. Falen, the most recent, is one I would recommend.)

In Pushkin's 'The Prophet', he speaks of the poet as a man whose lips God touches with the fire of truth. This is dangerous under any tyranny, and Pushkin himself was sent into exile in Southern Russia at 21, and was lucky to escape with his life a few years later when his friends were hanged in the unsuccessful Decembrist revolt. It was this aspect of Pushkin's life that made him an iconic figure, both for those who opposed the Tsar, and those who opposed the Soviet regime after the Tsars. Many took Pushkin's poetry into their prison camps as Evgenia Ginzburg attests, and in the long decades when Akhmatova was not allowed to publish her poetry she drew on Pushkin's verse for strength.

The first major poem of Pushkin I loved for myself was *The Gypsies*. This poem Pushkin wrote while he was in exile in Southern Russia, and much under the influence of Lord Byron. Unlike Byron, however, Pushkin was no tourist in the Caucasian regions he used as his setting. He had seen at first hand the nomadic Gypsies on the Bessarabian steppes, and knew the encampment he describes there:

> They sleep at peace under the skies
> Between the wheels of van and wagon
> Old carpets hang; their supper fries
> Upon an open fire; their horses
> Graze the bare field; behind the tent
> A tame bear sprawls at ease...

As so often in Pushkin's verse, it is the character of the central woman who is drawn with most energy. A Russian, Aleko, has fallen in love with Zemfira, whose taunting independence prefigures Bizet's Carmen. She gives Aleko her love for a time, but soon tires of him. Goaded by her readiness to admit she has fallen in love with another man, Aleko kills both Zemfira and her new lover. He is unpunished for the crime, but sent away by Zemfira's father in verse of resounding dignity. The Gypsies have no laws

> "To punish those who damage us
> But we don't live with murderers..."

Pushkin's popularity is of such magnitude in Russia that every government has found it necessary to have him on board. Even the Bolsheviks, who might have been expected to jettison Pushkin as an aristocratic irrelevance, chose instead to promote him as a noble victim of the Tsar...

A reader in the English literary tradition would have to imagine a poet with the sensuous richness of John Keats, the facility of Byron, and the bawdy obscenity of Chaucer. (His bawdy verses fit well in an issue of *Poetry Review* devoted to humour). Tsar Nikita and his forty daughters, is about forty princesses born without sexual organs. A messenger is sent to a local witch, who obligingly sends him back to the Court with a casket filled with suitable missing parts. Overcome by curiosity about the contents of the casket, the messenger shakes it, but can hear nothing. When he sniffs at it, however, he makes out "a familiar scent". Intrigued, he opens the box and to his horror, the forty female parts fly out like little birds, and settle on nearby trees. Nothing he does will coax them down again. Terrified at the likely result of returning to the Tsar with an empty casket, the messenger sits down where he is in despair until an old peasant woman, coming along the path, suggests a solution. He has simply to unveil his penis, and the female parts fly down and are easily caught. Another obscene poem, *The Gabrielad*, tells the story of the Annunciation in so dangerously offensive a way that Pushkin was forced to deny authorship at one period of his life.

These minor poems bear witness mainly to Pushkin's restless energies, which also found expression in the drawings in his working notebooks. Among his great poems must be counted *The Little Tragedies*, ably translated by Antony Wood. These were written in one of Pushkin's great autumns spent in Boldino towards the end of his life; the charm and economy of *Mozart and Salieri* evokes an unsuspicious, light-hearted victim much like Pushkin himself. Another superb poem, *The Bronze Horseman* conjures up both the frozen majesty of St Petersburg and the terror of a flood which wrecked the city in the 1820s. Pushkin catches both the drama of waves crashing through windows, and the pathos of pedlars trays floating on the waters. At the centre of the story is poor Evgeny, a clerk who dreams of marriage to his lovely Parasha. His misery at finding her house washed away sends him mad, and leads him to arraign the great Falconet statue of Peter the Great, the Tsar who built his capital below sea-level. What most readers will remember, however, is Evgeny's hallucination that the statue pursues him to his death, the metal hooves clattering on the cobbles of St Petersburg streets. It is an image and indeed a poem open to many interpretations.

Pushkin's popularity is of such magnitude in Russia that every government has found it necessary to have him on board. Even the Bolsheviks, who might have been expected to jettison Pushkin as an aristocratic irrelevance, chose instead to promote him as a noble victim of the Tsar, and to emphasize his love of folk lore and his peasant nanny.

As the bicentenary of his birth approaches in 1999, it is time for Pushkin to take his rightful place on the world stage: as triumphant an example of poetry victorious over this world's celebs as you will find. Anna Akhmatova has expressed that triumph most memoraby. "All the beauties, ladies in waiting, mistresses to the salons, Dames of the Order of St Catherine, members of the Imperial court, ministers, aides-de-camp, gradually began to be referred to as "contemporaries of Pushkin", and at length have been simply laid to rest (with their dates of birth and death garbled) in the indexes to editions of Pushkin's works".

Elaine Feinstein's biography, *Pushkin* (Weidenfeld & Nicholson, £20.00, ISBN 0 297 81826 0) is published this month.

ELAINE FEINSTEIN
PUSHKIN
EXEGI MONUMENTUM

I've set up for myself a monument, though not in stone.
No hands have made it, and no weeds will grow
Along the path to where the stubborn
    Head soars above Alexander's column.

I shall not die altogether. Lyrics of mine
Although my flesh decays, will hold my spirit
And I'll be known as long as any poet
    Remains alive under the moon.

News of me then will cross the whole of Russia
And every tribe there will have heard my name:
The Slavs, the Finns, and those in the wild Tungus,
    The Kalmucks on the plain.

And they will all love me, because my songs
Evoked some kindness in a cruel age,
Since I once begged for mercy to assuage
    The wrongs of the down fallen.

So, Muse, obey God's orders without fear
Forget insults, expect no laurel wreaths;
Treat praise and slander with indifference.
    And never argue with a fool.

Big Endians and Little Endians

HARRY CLIFTON ON A NEW ANTHOLOGY OF POST-45 POETRY

The Penguin Book of Poetry from Britain and Ireland since 1945

Edited by Simon Armitage
and Robert Crawford,
Viking, £25
ISBN 0 670 88325 5

TO BEGIN, SO to speak, in the middle. Irish reviewers, of whom I am one, will by now have become used to the existence of a new country called "And Ireland" that emerges like Surtsey out of the Atlantic each time an anthology of "these islands" is edited from the bigger of the two, which is almost always. We have heard of it before, we will be hearing of it again. Laws of proportion in "And Ireland" will be a source of amazement to poets and critics who lead waking lives in the state called Ireland, unless their name happens to be Jonathan Swift. Brobdingnagians at one end, Lilliputians at the other. Strange sabbaths of the dead, *à la* Sorley MacLean's 'Hallaig Wood', at which whole generations are glimpsed as in a mist, only to vanish again forever. And "far up in the right hand corner" as Brecht's famous poem of escape has it, a "small door can just be seen", leading to the realm of King Bloodaxe across the water, and a relative visibility in Britain.

But of all that, more in due course. Broader questions force themselves in beforehand. What, for instance, does "since 1945" mean in the context of poets born, as these are, between 1887 and 1965? What gap in anthology-space is this one supposed to fill? And finally, why now, so late in the century, with the big retrospectives just around the corner that will turn this collection into a side-issue almost before it is published? Let me emphasise – and I read every word of this anthology carefully and at leisure over a week – I have nothing against the poems themselves, of which it may be said in general that the "peripheries", be they Scottish, Irish, Caribbean or Indian, have moved in to fertilise the dead centre, a pattern now repeating itself on a larger scale in Western Europe. Good great and indifferent poems are here, many having migrated through successive ideologies or anthologies, and lived to tell their own tale. No, it is not the content that is wanting, it is any sense of definition.

"Examine this region", Auden writes in 'In Praise of Limestone', "of short distances and definite places". Had the editors used that as an epigraph, things mightn't have gotten so out of hand. As it is, they have ended up with two-and-a-half anthologies rolled into one. The first, where "time has done the sifting for us" has the Muirs, Audens, MacNeices, Thomases and Stevie Smiths. The second, a kind of modified Bloodaxe *New Poetry*, takes the story through from those born in the Forties. And there is, finally, a brief flutter on the horses of a Nineties Generation. Many of the poems here, right up to Don Paterson's 'A Private Bottling' from the Nineties, have been so endlessly-anthologised already one can only assume some entirely new constituency, or Amish-like wilderness sect, that remains to be wooed – which perhaps explains the babytalk of the introduction. "Almost everyone", it tells us, in Joyce Grenfell impersonation, "has written a poem at some time". Not to worry, though. Poetry "need not always be po-faced" or "embarrassing". As Pythonesque visions of tittering stockbrokers unwrapping *Since 1945* under Christmas trees crowd in, we are whisked onwards from Joyce Grenfell to Jacob Bronowski in masterful *Ascent of Man* mode. "What we now consider democracy was long and slow in evolving..." and we climb the evolutionary ladder, discarding Yeatsian pomp, Oxbridge *snobbisme* and Eliotish obscurity along the way. "The democratic voice was arriving".

With its arrival, allegedly around 1945, we reach the theoretical ground on which the editors wish to stand, such as it is. Multi-ethnic voices sing high and low on the social scale, all contributing to a vast Hiberno-Britannic polyphony where nothing excludes anything else. Everything is positive, everything is good. Omni-tolerance reigns, bar some dark asides about America. Which, of course, is ironic, since the basic model here is American, the horizontal spread of equality-with-difference rather than the vertical value-discriminatory code with its dangerous, or politically incorrect, notions of ethical, aesthetic or spiritual authenticity. It is no accident that Yeats is invoked as a predemocratic voice who sings "as if he had a sword upstairs". What seems to have been forgotten though, is that Yeats declared himself a democrat in politics, but not in art. Apparently, these editors want to be democrats in art as well, which leaves them with the hot potato of Poetic Value to rid themselves of as quickly as possible:

> While casting the net widely, we were conscious that all anthologists must face up to questions of poetic value. As a rule of thumb, four or five poems were selected from each of the poets who seemed to us particularly important in the period, with the hope that these selections would provide a spine for the anthology.

So that's that disposed of. With value reduced to a numbers game, we get back to being Democratic in earnest and preparing the Budget Day Speech: a sop to all potentially dangerous special interests, be they gender-based or language-based, be they Immigrant minorities or the Oxbridge/metropolitan set, whose shrill denunciation of the Bloodaxe *New Poetry* some years ago will have been kept in mind. As for the editors themselves, they are shamming dead ("...we thought it inappropriate to parade our own wares"), not unmindful, perhaps, of an *ad hominem* attack on editor Michael Hulse, whose own poems were included in *The New Poetry*. Ideological errors, too, are being corrected – Poetry is no longer, never was in fact, the new rock and roll. On Budget Day, in the parliament of democratic voices, nothing is being left to chance.

"This voice's emergence was heralded and later schooled by the Butler Education Act of 1944..." I doubt it. What about the social origins and poetic careers of Thomas Hardy or D. H. Lawrence? Are they not democratic voices? Is Stevie Smith's pre-war *A Good Time Was Had By All* radically different from her Fifties *Harold's Leap*? In what way is Auden's Thirties 'Miss Gee' different from post-1945 poems by Ruth Pitter or Wendy Cope, for example? Are the aforementioned Lawrence's Nottingham-dialect poems different from Blake Morrison's 'Yorkshire Ripper'? And so on. If it wasn't the democratic voices, then, was it the War that made 1945 some viable line of demarcation? There is little evidence of it in the poems included here, and some evidence to the contrary. For example Keith Douglas, surely Britain's finest war poet of those years, is nowhere to be seen in these pages, while Michael Longley and Ted Hughes have important and valuable poems pointing, instead, to the trauma of the First World War. More importantly Auschwitz, after which, the editors tell us, "poetry was subtly different than before" is an indicator. Bar Karen Gershon, with her one conventional lyric, there is no one here with an experience of the Holocaust direct enough to modify consciousness or idiom, as happened with the postwar poets of Eastern Europe. Instead we have the well-mannered and honourably-intentioned 'Formal Elegies' of W. H. Auden, Peter Porter, Geoffrey Hill or James Fenton, writing in what the *Ecrits des Condamnées à Mort* described as "pre-war modes" about war-time or post-war trauma. A further illustration of how this "subject", even when not directly felt, can still be used, is Sylvia Plath's questionable appropriation of it ("An engine, an engine / Chuffing me off like a Jew.. . / I think I may well be a Jew") in 'Daddy', included here, as fuel for a personal animus. A defining episode in European consciousness seems to have passed British poetics by, and almost incidentally, given the lie to any predication, at least in poetry, of a pre- and post-1945 divide.

Inadequate though the Auschwitz poems may be, they do show one thing – the continued prevalence of what Al Alvarez, in his well-known introduction to *The New Poetry* of nearly forty years ago, called the Gentility principle, that very British cultivation of a middle range of feeling, of moderation to the point of lifelessness. We seem to have come full-circle from the doctrine of extremity propounded in that volume, through various detours like the *Children of Albion* and the *Conductors of Chaos*, to a renewed doctrine of harmlessness. The postwar New Apocalyptics – about whom I would have liked to have known more – clearly don't fit the "democratic voices" bill and are hastily glided over. A great age of songwriting and rap, perhaps too dangerously real and close to the street, goes unrepresented, bar such as Linton Kwesi Johnston or Benjamin Zephaniah who have been filtered through the acceptability-mechanism of mainstream publishing. On the other hand, the middle ground has incubated its own Guilt Complex – and I don't mean Conscience, I mean Guilt Complex – in the shape of Peter Reading, "who has worked as a lecturer and crane operator", and whose interminable 'Ukelele Music', reproduced at length in these pages, fails to conceal beneath its would-be uglifications a thoroughgoing aesthete and sentimentalist. Reading, for all his excremental anti-poetry, is simply the gentility principle turned inside out.

As for "those two geographical entities, Britain and Ireland", whose "mutual awareness remains throughout unarguable", a little history is in order. In the Fifties, with the establishment of Dolmen Press in Ireland, and later, in the Seventies and Eighties, through the Irish Arts Councils and presses such as Daedalus, Gallery, Raven Arts/New Island, Blackstaff and Salmon, a concept known as The Repatriation of Irish Poetry arose, whose catchphrase was "Irish poets need never again look to London for publishing outlets". What was forgotten, unfortunately, was that London had stopped looking too, with results that have been all too evident, in anthologies such as this, ever since. Out of sight was out of mind. Which would not matter if, as these editors assert, "ideas of absolute central authority" had "dissolved", and compilations like this or its predecessor the Bloodaxe *New Poetry* or others to come were edited on a democratic basis from both sides of the water. Clearly that hasn't happened, and as long as Britain continues to be the editorial centre, Irish poetry will find itself being defined for itself from outside itself and prescribed to itself through the superior distributive mechanisms of Penguin and others, and institutionalised into Irish academic courses where students, thinking they are reading about real Ireland, will be reading about "And Ireland" instead. That may be an outcome of many things – a failure of Irish publishers to get their message across, or an unbridgeable divide between two psychic realities – but democracy it certainly is not.

So, to the democratic chorus stopping short – bar an odd lyric by a Kennelly, a Meehan, a Sirr – at the Irish border, let me append a few names. Samuel Beckett and Francis Stuart, both authors of small but crucial bodies of work spanning the War and its spiritual aftermath. The lifework of Padraig Fallon. John Montague, appointed to the Chair of Irish Poetry, whose *Collected Poems* appeared two years ago. Michael Hartnett, who has midwived

elements of this and the previous Bloodaxe anthology, only to be excluded from both. The antiphonal northern voices of James Simmons and Seamus Deane. A whole range of Gaelic poets, from Mairtin O'Direain, Sean O'Riordain, Biddy Jenkinson, Gabriel Rosenstock and Michael Davitt, through to Cathal O'Searcaigh and Louis de Paor, not to mention the bilingual Pearse Hutchinson. The Old and New World oscillations of Eamon Grennan. The nature-mysticism of Dermot Healy. The Meath re-rootings of Peter Fallon and the Italian travellings of Macdara Woods. The rough strength of John Ennis. The Other-European irony and lyricism of Dennis O'Driscoll and Michael O'Loughlin. The love-and-politics of Thomas McCarthy, whose 'Emigration Trains', a paradigm of the fate of millions of Irish in Britain, cries out for inclusion in a book like this:

> We were heading for England and the world
> At war. Neutrality we couldn't afford.
> I thought I would spend two years away
> But in the end the two became twenty.
> Within hours we'd reach the junction at Crewe
> And sample powdered eggs from the menu,
> As well as doodlebugs falling nearby;
> All that fatal traffic of an alien sky.

All these, and many more – Gerald Dawe, Aidan Matthews, Julie O'Callaghan, Pat Boran, Moya Cannon, Kerry Hardie or Gerard Fanning, for instance – have distinct identities within Irish poetry. Of a younger generation coming through, Justin Quinn, Sinead Morrissey, Conor O'Callaghan, Vona Groarke and David Wheatley could easily have taken the place of the weaker brethren at the tail-end of this anthology. And – one final observation in this regard – of Northern Irish inclusions, Seamus Heaney, Michael Longley and Paul Muldoon are all represented by up-to-date work, while Derek Mahon, whose last two books were published in Ireland, might as well have died twenty years ago. He has been repatriated into invisibility. Faced with this latest evidence of the limitations of an Irish publishing strategy, Irish poets – the younger ones in particular – would do well to consider their position. Because clearly, for all the plausible talk here of mutuality and decentralisation, certain realities are not going to change.

Democracy, even in so innocuous a form as an anthology like this, has a way of concealing its own power-bases, even from itself, and seeming to be more even-handed than it actually is. If I appear to concentrate on one area of omission, it is because I believe that, on this side of the water at least, no-one else will even notice it. The only advice I will give, then, is a slight variant on the usual recommendations where anthologies are concerned. Ignore the introduction, read the poems, and if you're Irish – from Ireland, that is, not "And Ireland" – read the silences as well.

CHARLES TOMLINSON
FIRE AND AIR

Silk scarves of flame
wind from the coals
liquidly leaping them to and fro,
uncircling whichever way aircurrents go.

They aim to join
the airstream flowing above the house,
disordering every tree,
that lures them upwards into nonentity.

Strange, that opposites
should reach for the same
unassailable altitude
as if air and fire were a single flame.

As they are
when a house burns down
and they race the stairway, lit
by the one desire to have done with it,

leaving a silhouette
blackened behind them,
cardboard cut-out where once was wall,
swaying unflamelike, tottering to downfall.

A truce on the hearth tonight
keeps all in peace, in place,
mingling fire and air beyond blame.
Do not cease to admire such a scene. Do not trust a flame.

Poetry Place in Space

by David Wheatley

GWYNETH LEWIS

Zero Gravity

Bloodaxe, £6.95.
ISBN 1 85224 456 9

IN RECENT YEARS we've had poets in residence in Marks and Spencer's, London Zoo and even Barnsley Football Club, but as the third millennium approaches, the world still awaits its first writer in space. Granted, crowds might be difficult to attract to readings out there, but it still seems unfair when you consider how much poetry space has inspired, from Plato to John Donne to Edwin Morgan. If NASA ever does get together with the National Endowment for the Arts, one name they should keep in mind is the latest addition to this constellation of talents, Gwyneth Lewis. There can't be many other poets on this year's Forward shortlist with an astronaut in the family: the title sequence of *Zero Gravity* was inspired by her American cousin's voyage on the Space Shuttle as part of the mission to repair the Hubble telescope.

The sequence has already been widely praised – Lewis being the sort of poet who picks up her back-of-the-book quotations before her collections are published, leaving the mere reviewer looking rather superfluous – but in this case the hype can be safely endorsed. Its sixteen short sections make a highly impressive piece of work, twining together her cousin's Hubble mission and an elegy for her sister-in-law. Describing the dying woman's illness, Lewis discovers a sort of poetic Doppler effect: "It must be that pain // accelerates something. / Her speeding mind / leaves us in the present, / a long way behind" while her cousin carries his helmet "like a severed head. / We think of you as already dead". When Derek Mahon began his great poem 'A Disused Shed in Co. Wexford' with the line "Even now there are places where a thought might grow" he was looking forward to poems like this.

It was Sean O'Brien who said that all poems about cats are twee, even poems about drowning them. An even bigger danger than tweeness in animal poems is anthropomorphization, turning them into poems about humans instead. Lewis skil-fully avoids both these dangers in 'The Booming Bittern' and 'Prayer for Bandy', a poem about having her dog put to sleep. The latter in particular is one of the highlights of this collection:

> I held his breath in the palm of my hand,
> fresh as a flower. Rest easy now.
> He gave us our capacity
> for loving him. Original sin
>
> in dogs must be biting. Take pity on him
> for being doggy, for not understanding
> we don't do that here. We hope
> he forgave us for killing him.

Empathizing with her dog shouldn't be much of a problem for Lewis, since elsewhere in the book she's imagining a man as a wardrobe and comparing a woman to "a *chaise* / he yearns to be *longue* on" ('The Love of Furniture'). It's all part of the same metaphysical imagination we saw in 'Six Poems on Nothing' in *Parables & Faxes*, lifting her flights of fancy beyond the orbit of hand-me-down Martianism into full-blown conceits. Other examples would include 'Talk with a Headache', a neuralgic rewriting of 'Mary Had a Little Lamb', and 'The Pier', an elegy for Joseph Brodsky.

These days poets are falling over themselves to post their work on the internet, but few are writing about information technology as well as Lewis in poems like 'Communications' and 'Website Future' with its megabytes and e-mail: "No need for me once we're on the net, / are a wave to be surfed on, have gone world-wide. / No awkward engines to curate / but templates which never knew a tide". Her technological know-how may come from working as a television producer, but elsewhere in the same poem she comes out with as pre-digitally unforgettable a line as anyone could ask for: "Unforecast snow falls softly in our hearts".

A final indication of how good Lewis is: the number of perfectly good poems she's published in magazines since *Parables & Faxes* but hasn't collected here. What did she think was wrong with 'The Art of Swearing' and 'Twins', two favourites of mine? The second of these turns on the use of the *chi* or "thou" form in Welsh, reminding us that, aside from the two books she's given us in English, Lewis is also the author of a collection in Welsh, *Sonedau Redsa*. Perhaps she'd translate it for us? If it's half as good as *Zero Gravity* it's already half way towards being as good as they come.

Jazzmen, Europhiles and Homicides

BY SHEENAGH PUGH

NEIL POWELL

Selected Poems

Carcanet, £8.95
ISBN 1 85754 350 5

ALISON FELL

Dreams, Like Heretics: New & Selected Poems

Serpent's Tail, £8.99
ISBN 1 85242 561 X

DUNCAN BUSH

The Hook

Seren, £7.95
ISBN 1 855411 203 1

JEREMY HOOKER

Our Lady of Europe

Enitharmon, £8.95
ISBN 1 900564 15 7

GRAHAM MORT

Circular Breathing

Dangaroo Press, £7.95
ISBN 1 871049 43 1

I STARTED WITH Powell because be was the only one I hadn't come across before. Why, I wonder? "Ignorance, Madam; pure ignorance" ... but really it's down to the fact that there are so many poets published nowadays, and some are more hyped than others. Some poets can't cough without provoking a critical article, and some just publish for thirty-odd years relatively unremarked, and the difference is not always one of talent.

I enjoyed a lot about Powell; the wry humour of lust – "the dry-cleaner's son is ruining my life"; the way the whole collection revolves around friends who recur, sometimes as dedicates, sometimes,

later, as subjects of elegies, which is curiously upsetting, as if we'd already come to know them. Within limits, I also like the phrasemaking. He is extremely polished at that; handling rhyme and form fluently. This can be very readable and easy to memorise – 'A Cambridge House', quoted in full:

> Suddenly space: high ceilings and white walls.
> Perhaps I thought a change would set me right –
> Simple as that. False logic of façades,
> An each-way bet, a love at second sight,
> The liar's self-conviction of a truth:
> Thus caution tempts desire to leasehold life.
> Bland architectural graces, signs misread.
> Within, some space stayed uninhabited.

At times, though, I'm ungrateful enough to feel it sounds too fluent, too easy. He's very fond of iambics, particularly iambic pentameter. I'm not usually one of those who moan about this: the iamb is the base rhythm of English adult speech and when I read poets praised for liberating themselves from it, the first thing I notice is how easily dactyls and anapaests can resemble a childish jingle. But iambic pentameter can get monotonous, and I think his does. There is a complex fifteen-sonnet sequence, 'A Cooling Universe' (the fifteenth sonnet is made up of the first lines of the previous fourteen, and the last line of each is the first of the next). It's a technical triumph, but the rhythms are so regular and flowing that it nearly sent me to sleep.

I tried my best with the jazz poems, I really did... Many poets seem to write about jazz; perhaps jazz poems are more fun to write than to read. They never recreate the music, and for non-fans they are excluding, full of names which mean more to the writer than to the reader. I must curb my own itch to write about C & W.

Alison Fell

Powell's *Selected Poems* is based on several collections over 30 years, which seems reasonable. Alison Fell's is an amalgam of two collections and some new poems, which doesn't. Presumably she didn't have enough for a new collection. She is mainly a prose writer, us many of these poems make clear. Too many unshaped ideas, even quotations, are sitting around pretending to be poems –

> There's no word for the feeling women
> have of being in the wrong before
> they even open their months,

Dale Spender says
(' Significant Fevers')

So if Spender has already said this in decent prose, why must Fell repeat it in chopped-up prose with pointless line breaks? What kind of unit of sense or sound is "have of being in the wrong before"? Anyone who hears that as a line of poetry should certainly be writing prose.

She likes telling us who said what – again from 'Significant Fevers':

Levi-Strauss, if I understand him right,
says that women disrupt the man-made
opposition between nature and culture

and, from 'Kisses for Mayakovsky':

Mayakovsky said
"One must tear happiness
from the days to come".

The trouble is, I see no reason to read her version rather than the original, and the same goes for her reworkings of myth and legend; they don't alter or transcend anything. The epigraph of "A tender youth without fault or blemish" is a sentence of unforgettable eighth-century Irish prose, hut the poem appended slips quite easily from memory.

The later love-and-loss poems have some memorable moments, notably 'Le Poisson de Bonheur':

is it like the sea breathing,
the way you reach for nothing, know

no separation
from the great body of radiance?

But the tone is inconsistent; there are *Woman's Own*ish moments like "when you crushed me to you" ('Thalassa') and, ending that poem, some unintended humour:

if you swore you would come
back again and again
to our own sweet bed
to heave gladly
at its oars...

It's that line break, again; before my eye travelled down to "at its oars", I thought he was retching,

and now I can't get that picture out of my head. There's not enough here for a *Selected*, but what there is still needs pruning.

Duncan Bush

Duncan Bush has produced a sort of partial *Selected*, a reissue of poems from three collections now out of print. For those who already have these, the incentive to buy is that he has revised some of them – this is the remix, so to speak. (Will he eventually produce a full-scale *Selected*, with remixes of the remixes, and get the reader to fork out a third time?)

If you're a Bush fan, it is for the ideas, which have always predominated; he is a cerebral writer whose thought ranges widely, a translator with a pan-European mindset. Following his thought process can be exciting, especially when he finds live images to clothe it in, as in 'Gothic Cathedral':

The round-shouldered stone
cuneiforms

that held the arc
bowed down by

weight unhooped and lifted
to acuteness;

growing tall, they earthed mass.
The load

passed into the ground
like electricity

along green copper.
Glasswork

broke the rainbow's
arch into

its parts and brought
them
in

The line breaks, though, make no kind of sense, and indeed I've always felt that if I could hear more rhythm and music in his work, it would be more memorable – I've never managed to learn one by heart. Neil Powell's rhythms may sometimes flow too smoothly and regularly, but at least they're there.

Jeremy Hooker

Jeremy Hooker is another Europhile and this collection's range includes Wales, the Netherlands, France, Belgium, Spain, Greece and Israel (well, they enter the Eurovision Song Contest). There is actually enough here for another *Selected*, and for a single collection I found its size and scope a bit daunting: I'd just about got into one country when, like a tour bus on a tight schedule, we were off to the next.

Hooker admits himself, in 'Homage to René Char', "I have been inclined to pick up images like stones" and sometimes he has been content to name the objects he uses for material, rather than shaping them. There are many lists of objects here:

> Olives, of course. And cypresses.
> And waste ground littered with bottles,
> rusted iron, oil drums.
> A carrion crow picking over it
> ('Jerusalem Sketchbook')

> Thistles, poppies, blue cranesbill
> by a dusty road
> In front, under the cloud stack
> of an August sky,
> the chalk ridge
> ('Verdun')

They work best, as he says himself, when they contain shaping force. Take 'Strata Florida (2)', 1 don't know whether, in the repeated reference to "your red hair, your grey hair", I am meant to hear the echo of Celan's refrain from the *Todesfuge*, but I do, and what the poem has to say about love and ageing becomes more 3-D because of it. This, incidentally, is one free-verse poet who could never be accused of writing prose in lines.

Graham Mort

Two striking things about *Circular Breathing*: Mort's interest in shady, nay homicidal characters, and his non-judgmental attitude to most of them. 'A Quiet Bloke' is a murderer; the 'Quarryman' an abusive husband, but they are also human and capable of evoking sympathy. The "you" of 'Black Market' is about to be a hit-man, but the way his descent is chronicled leaves you feeling it could have happened to anyone really. A line in 'A Riddle for the Serbian Wars' could be emblematic for this collection, with its refusal to categorise anyone as sub-human: "I am the poem in a rapist's mouth". Radovan Karadzic has claims to be a poet; the late great Vasko Popa really was one, and some of his beautiful "Serbian wolf" imagery reads alarmingly when you think who might now be carrying it about in their heads.

Mort's poetry has a strong narrative element, and sometimes the narrative line is more obscure than I like it – maybe I'm just lazy. I was never wholly sure what was going on in 'Wall Riders' and 'A House of Glass', nor to whom 'Laxton's Superb' is addressed (lover? But they live in the same childhood house. Sibling? Then why "your father"?) And there are, as in most collections, a few poems ('Southbound', 'Fox') which don't look as if they urgently needed to be written. But most of the book consists either of these intriguingly disturbing personae or, interspersed with them, a series of thoughtful, sometimes painful love poems chronicling a relationship which, though flawed, difficult and interrupted, seems in the end to survive. At least, the last poem, 'Words', ends

> You'll forget tonight
> But it doesn't matter, we'll die anyhow,
> it matters that we feel the hurt of loving now.

Through a Glass Darkly

by David Kennedy

ANNE CARSON

Glass and God

Cape, £8.00
ISBN 0 224 051172

CANADIAN POET ANNE Carson's first UK collection comes trailing some impressive recommendations. For Michael Ondaatje, she is "the most exciting poet writing in English today" and for Peter Porter "a new and brilliant talent". One thing which differentiates Carson's work is its level of ambition, which is evidenced by its particular combination of cultural literacy and lack of fear of thinking. The other is that the poetry always seems to be on the verge of prose – the final section 'Short Talks' is a sequence of short prose pieces – so that it makes more sense to think of the contents of *Glass and*

God not as poetry but as species of text works. This is part of the book's ambition but it also means that its challenges and rewards are located in areas such as pattern, narrative and what one might term viral referencing. Here's the start of the opening sequence 'The Glass Essay':

I can hear little clicks inside my dream.
Night drips its silver tap
down the back.
At 4 A.M. I wake. Thinking

of the man who
left in September.
His name was Law.

My face in the bathroom
mirror
has white streaks down it.
I rinse the face and return
to bed.
Tomorrow I am going to
visit my mother.

The cool, self-brutalizing stare of confessional poetry is certainly present here but it is deftly shadowed by an ironizing knowingness. The passage is a little too in love with how many changes it can ring on its "i" and "a" sounds, and how seriously are we to take the second stanza which seems to allude to the clichés of popular song and in which feminist allegory is left deliberately ambiguous? "His name was Law" almost invites us to groan and say "O yeah, and I bet his best mate was Pat Riarchy". Carson's style may be plain but it is not crude. As the sequence develops into a gripping and, at times, moving narrative it becomes clear that these three stanzas function as a thematic kernel. 'The Glass Essay' becomes, amongst other things, an account of the protagonist's grieving over and recovery from her love affair, an exploration of her relationship with her mother and her hospitalised father, and a sort of critical essay on Emily Brontë. Brontë's life and work come to stand for not just for the inner life of women but for wider questions about the possibility of self-knowledge. In this context, the sequence's title functions as a simultaneous image and mockery of the transparency of

> The compressive demands of form allow a focus on what Bernard O'Donoghue refers to in Muldoon as "exterior metonymic structure". The result is that the repetition of words and images mime the kind of jump cuts and slippages that characterise the actualities of mental activity. 'The Glass Essay' is a suggestive demonstration of poetry's ability to present the inner world of feeling and thinking and the outer world of fact as matters of process and revisiting.

our inner and outer lives to ourselves.

Now, of course, all this raises the question of why Anne Carson bothered to write this as poetry. It would have worked equally well as fiction or as the type of autobiographical critical theorising that has recently become popular in North America. Part of the answer is that poetry allows the imagination and more analytic thinking to be susceptible to each other in ways that other cultural forms do not. The compressive demands of form allow a focus on what Bernard O'Donoghue refers to in Muldoon as "exterior metonymic structure". The result is that the repetition of words and images mime the kind of jump cuts and slippages that characterise the actualities of mental activity. 'The Glass Essay' is a suggestive demonstration of poetry's ability to present the inner world of feeling and thinking and the outer world of fact as matters of process and revisiting.

The ambition and achievement of 'The Glass Essay' are not, however, sustained in the remainder of *Glass and God*. Four sequences – 'The Truth About God', 'T. V. Men', 'The Fall of Rome: A Traveller's Guide' and 'Short Talks' – attempt to make the cool exactitudes and critical insights of 'The Glass Essay' ends in themselves. This works best in 'The Fall of Rome' which has fun with phrasebooks and modern Roman manners but the three other sequences seem uninvolving. This is unfortunate because the book wants to ponder questions similar to Heaney's "Where does spirit live? Inside or outside...?" In this it continues the Cape list's unstated project to explore the possibilities of a spiritual, broadly Christian poetry in an age when even words like "God" and "holiness" are unlikely to evoke emotional responses in a majority of readers. Carson counters this with a detached, philosophical approach but her attempts at parables, latter-day koans and resonant oddities read largely like penultimate drafts. Without the patterns and returns of 'The Glass Essay' her work seems deprived of energy.

SMITA AGARWAL
ARRIVAL

Within this hotel room,
at this point in time,
I stand beside him.

Under the tail lancet window,
through stained glass,
I see heat waves rise;
He – forests of black pine.

Some hundred feet below us,
on the busy motorway,
red double-decker coaches
appear to him – blue.

Now will we turn to face this room?

In the far left corner
a plush burgundy bed
(we'll sink into);
leopard-skin sofa;
a fawn-coloured carpet
(tickles the soles of my naked feet);
Straight-backed chairs, two;
a four-cornered winking eye,
softly blathering news . . .

When will I mention the lace-covered,
lion's paw table, tucked away on my right?

On it, long-stemmed glasses,
bottles of wine, cheeses,
a statuette of Rodin's *The kiss,*
a bowl of fruit . . .

And the missing champagne bottle,
will on its own uncork, froth, spew,
when, into some other room I walk in,
at another point in time,
clutching to my bosom
a swaddled little-boy-blue?

PAUL HENRY
HOLIDAY HOME

This house, built on clay, the last
to slide into the sea,
splits its sides with parting cracks
by those who signed the book:

the Burns of Slough, 1959 –
"This Shangri-La of Wales must never die!" . . .

Dunkirk's very own
Dot & Ken, June '65 –
"Flymo broken. Shears first class!" . . .

and, lest we forget, *"Rex The P-o-ET!"*
whose pawprint authenticates
some doggerel from 1972 . . .

The Burns return in '86, retired,
smug, children's professions listed
as if it counted – Accountant, G. P. ,
Lawyer and . . . one missing
from *"Our Infamous Four!"*

Thirty-nine summers

assembled and folded away
neatly, into a fractured box,
like jigsaws, cards or dominoes

lined up purely to be felled
by the tide, which raises the stakes
with each turned over wave.

Here's the owner, Spring '98:
Hilary B – *"Down for repairs,
to keep this place afloat!"*

I take in her skewed watercolours
and books, half-comforted
that someone still flies with Biggles,

pedals, bare-kneed, to Smuggler's Top
up the stairwell's 1 in 1.

Happy to sleep, to squat
almost imperially
on these suspect foundations,

I turn in the same, creaking lie
as those who signed its sheets
eloquently, with love,

whose breakages, like mine,
are paid for by the sea's refrain –

Come back . . . come back . . . come back . . .

DERYN REES-JONES
SPELLS

I

The bed becomes a page, the white sheets
Where we leave ourselves,
Hair, fluids, sloughed off skin,
Cells of the self grown out of themselves
Not living but unchanged, as any lover's history.
And here, like a wing, or a sycamore seed
Is the L of my arm, and here is my hand
On your halo of hair. I want to spell out all
The harboured messages of joy, make an alphabet
Of our hands and bodies, rewrite our movements,
Make everything strange. To speak what is us,
What is you, or me; each vowel, each consonant,
Now coded in the silent movements of our sleep.

I I

The vowels, the consonants of speech, sound wrong
Because like all translators we have failed. We learn to misread
Or adequately speak, the words that waltz, cavort or slip,
Terrible on the starry page. Instead, we're left with all the painful
Ghostings of ourselves. *Her voice* in another language, the way you say
His eyes. And words as unaccountable to things as love.

And memories slither. And thoughts collide.
When we dream it is ice that we dream of, and snow.
When you say that you love me, you say it in sleep.
We're all of us dying but I want this to live.
Our days collapse, the nights draw in. A smudge of mouth
A flurry of hands. Even the darkness is crying out
Through the pale O of your dreaming mouth.

I I I

Your soft mouth says my name,
Makes me unfamiliar, makes me look at myself
From a distance again. But
The soft V of my breasts that I find
When at last you take hold of me, puts me to flight.
And this flight's still a bird's, or an echo of bird
As softly I push into you, feathering your eyelids
With my tongue, strobing a cool sandpapery cheek.
And when I write of myself,
It is now as a 2, our joined lives
Make the shape of a swan. *What makes as afraid?*
Beside us in the emerald water
The swan's white reflection.

I V

Your long body is a history I want to find a way to read
Negotiating bends and swan-like corners,
The map of constellations on your back, the isthmus
Of your ankle, the wayward hill of your contoured chest,
Peaks of your buttocks, lovely knees.
I try to read you backwards, frontways,
From top to bottom, right to left. I whisper in morse
To colour your dreams, then signal my errors,
Eight semaphore Es. And if love is a mirror I see only your face
And if love is a window I tap at the glass. If I licked you alive,
Would the whole summer warm me? My sighs are spells,
They are gasps for breath. The question-mark of your loving body
Rousing me at last to speech.

ANN SANSOM
PRINCE

for Andrew Stibbs

I study the board like the rules of a dead language
to be repeated, memorised, tried on the edge of the tongue
but not applied, not usefully, not at this time of night
with the last train shunted out and the porters absent,
cosy, brewing up behind their mirrored door.

Snowed in once, they offered me a drop of whisky
in a mug of orange tea. Not tonight
because rain's a different element;
no camaraderie for those who're wet and late,
victims of their own persistent gullibility.

That time, at least I had a book, Machiavelli.
I read it twice. The station stray snored
at my feet. I got organised and ruthless overnight,
learned how human affairs are governed;
above all else, be wary of benevolent advice.

Tonight it's the *Rotherham Star* or nothing,
fragile and damp from the bin. Letters, small ads,
garden fork, one tine missing, excellent condition
Massage and Sauna for Business Gents,
Adult Videos, a double spread of Lonely Hearts.

The realpolitik: *fortune is changeable like a woman*
or an April timetable *but a man of goodwill is obstinate
and usefully predictable,* a snooty dog that comes to heel.
Good boy. At least I know your name.

Augustan Humours

By Richard Tyrrell

JOHN HEATH-STUBBS

The Literary Essays

ed. Trevor Tolley
Carcanet £14.95
ISBN 1 85754 352 1

POETS WHO STILL read Latin and the Italian of Tasso and Ariosto are not exactly thick on the ground. Still fewer are those familiar with Edmund Spenser's astrological calendar, the gothic influence of *Vathek* by William Beckford (who?), and the philosophy of Mark Akenside's *Pleasures of the Imagination*. John Heath-Stubbs's familiarity with the unfamiliar is one of the fascinations of his essays. As a diligent educator, he rarely writes about a poet without a heap of detail about the poet's period, life, political and literary affiliations, and sources. Hence, he is able to suggest at least three roots for T. S. Eliot's famously enigmatic "three white leopards [that] sat under a juniper-tree" – in Goethe, Grimm, and George MacDonald. He tells us that he once questioned Eliot directly about his sources. But what he found was the same ambivalence that the student got who asked what the white-leopard lines meant, only to have Old Possum read the lines back to him.

A section of *The Literary Essays* – published to coincide with Heath-Stubb's 80th birthday – is devoted to modern poets. But it's difficult to escape the feeling that those who really set his pulses racing are the Augustans. As far back as 1948, he wrote:

The so-called Augustan Age ... represents one of those rare moments in history when perfection of style is achieved. This perfection symbolizes the momentary triumph of civilisation and the human intellect over that chaos which lies eternally around and within us.

As if to underscore the point, Heath-Stubbs then proves he is as worth reading on this period as Eliot was on the Elizabethans. We are still living, as he frequently points out, in the Romantic backwash to the Augustans, in which individuality is prized more highly than shared cultural norms; but poets today (in the light of the new formalism) will probably respond more warmly to the strengths Heath-Stubbs brings to light – their self-control, their humanising of the imagination, their argument with the irrational and disruptive elements in it. It is the classicism and cliched adjectives of the Augustans that often tire modern readers. But Heath-Stubbs – in a *tour-de-force* essay on Thomas Gray – is excellent in helping us make adjustments: "With regard to the adjective, we have come to expect it sharply to particularise the noun it qualifies. But to Gray ... its function is rather to define the general and persistent quality of a thing". In the Tasso essay, Heath-Stubbs discusses the centrality of epic poetry, which largely explains his high opinion of Landor's epic poem, *Gebir*, but also indirectly his own attempt – via his lyrics and epic, Artorius – to revive a classical consciousness in modern poetry.

As a critic, he falls within Eliot's description: he commends, explains, illuminates under-rated poetry, understands how a poem is of its time or outside it. He is also consistent. In an essay of 1948, for instance, he alludes to Edgar Allan Poe as a "crude imitator of certain features of Shelley's work". In a later lecture in 1988, he tactfully refrains from evaluating Poe's poetry, preferring to focus for the sake of his American audience on the fiction, while noting that Poe treated verse as a form of metronomic science. There is a lot of generosity in this determination to embrace the best in a writer, while keeping a tight rein on the internal censor.

The Literary Essays are not fully representative of Heath-Stubbs's criticism. It contains nothing from his 1950 book, *The Darkling Plain*, which examined the 1830's poets. A few of the essays, such as that on Shelley, could be meatier; his essay on Swift (from 1948) would no doubt be fuller if written today, especially after Nokes's biography. Given his range of interests, the book cries out for something on William Blake, who is tantalisingly mentioned in several key places. Not everyone will agree with the assessment of Auden – over-rated, often metrically flaccid, drifting on the currents of his age without saying anything original (a sort of 20th century Tennyson) – but one can see his point. It is fair to say that Heath-Stubbs makes all his points with supreme erudition. He leaves us with a desire to re-read the poets – and there is no better compliment to criticism than that.

From the Yorkshire

by Roy Hattersley

SIMON ARMITAGE

All Points North

Viking, £14.99
ISBN 0 67087 300 4

MY IRRITATION MAY be the product of resentment. Simon Armitage writes with self-confident familiarity of places which I know and love, so reading *All Points North* arouses all the emotions which I felt when Len Hutton, my boyhood hero, visited the house of a youth I barely knew. But, self-criticism not being one of the habits which I acquired in post-war Yorkshire, I must consider the possibility that my reservations result from judgement rather than jealousy. In his desperate desire to separate sentiment from sentimentality, Armitage is too often mannered. Half of the narrative is written in the second person. A chapter which begins "Driving around looking for a house to buy, you stray over the top into Lancashire..." has a clear subtext. It reads "the writer has a number of endearing reminiscences about the West Riding which he writes in a style that he hopes will confirm that his work has literary merit".

> Perhaps Armitage did turn up his television set when he heard a headboard banging against the wall of the next room of his Nassau hotel. It is even, possible that the banging was his neighbour registering his complaint about the noise that the television was making. But I first heard the story thirty years ago.

The other half of *All Points North* is written with an endearing simplicity which makes the conceits and the contrivances all the more annoying. When the amateur dramatic society assembles for its trip to Bridlington "one man cracks open a can of beer and his wife shakes her head in despair. A woman in a spangly gold blouse and leggings pours tea from a flask and offers the cup round". The claim that "we couldn't really be from anywhere else other than Yorkshire" may be impossible to justify. But as the description of the day goes on Armitage constructs a perfect vignette of West Riding respectability. The coach "pulls on to the gravel forecourt of a truck-stop, one passenger describes the café as a greasy spoon. 'It's a road house', his wife corrects him. 'I'll have tea and an orange KitKat'".

That was a story from the Armitage boyhood. It is when he grows up that he develops problems with style. The grammatical errors are excusable. Perhaps the "fat boy sat on a garden wall" had been forcibly placed there by an angry football enthusiast – who resented being asked to pay a hundred pounds for what should have cost only thirty. Anyway, we always confuse our tenses in Yorkshire and Armitage's lapse into the local patois adds veracity to his story. Much better that than the style he adopts to describe preparing to read poems to a Sixth Form College. "Beforehand you are writing out a list of poems to read..." My immediate reaction to the affectation of that opening sentence is "Oh no I'm not". Which (adopting Armitage's rejection of verbs) is a pity. The story that follows – fiction or fictitious – is well worth repeating.

So indeed are most of Armitage's anecdotes. He is particularly good at dog stories – even those which are not trite but have "been told so many times you started to believe it. happened to you" (a proper northern use of the second person in preference to the nauseous southern posh "one"). I particularly liked the one about the Alsatian which followed him into a house he was visiting and "after about half an hour got up and crapped in the corner and then sat back down by the fire". After an unsuccessful attempt to ignore the incident, Armitage asked why the dog was not made to go outside – only to be told "It's not my dog. I thought it was yours". Good as the story is, the description of the defecation needs some explanation. Do they really talk about crapping in modern Yorkshire? In my young days we were either more genteel or more Anglo-Saxon. But that was before Britain had capitulated to the American cultural invasion.

Armitage was born, and to his credit still lives, in a very special part of Yorkshire. The Colne Valley, which is more of an area than a geographical feature, paradoxically straddles the Pennines. When, long ago, I hoped to be the Labour parliamentary candidate for that constituency, I was disconcerted to find that some of the electors whom I would have to woo and win actually lived in Lancashire. It was, back in 1962, still "a hot bed of radical thought and political activism" but had already fallen "into a long pleasant afternoon nap". One of the most energetic members of the local Labour Party was called Gladstone Mather. It was not until he told me that he owed his Christian name to a birthday which coincided with the Grand Old Man's first election victory that I realised that he was ninety four. Such people may exist in the south. But down there they are less proud of them,

Like *Coronation Street* – a comparison which the author will probably resent – *All Points North* is at its worst when it moves out of its natural habitat. 'Tour of Duty', two and a half pages of an account of an American excursion, is a rag-bag of stories which are too hackneyed to be funny. Perhaps Armitage did turn up his television set when he heard a headboard banging against the wall of the next room of his Nassau hotel. It is even, possible that the banging was his neighbour registering his complaint about the noise that the television was making. But I first heard the story thirty years ago. It has no place in an anthology which clearly claims some literary merit. 'Mum's Gone to Iceland'

succeeds where 'All Points' fails because. although the action takes place in Reykjavik, the characters are pure Marsden, Milnsbridge and Slaithwaite.

Most anthologies – and all collections which bring together old work and new – mix the good, the bad and the makeweight. *All Points North* suffers from the author's inability to make up his mind what sort of Yorkshire he wants to celebrate. Mercifully it is certainly not the West Riding of Hovis advertisements – all cloth caps, racing pigeons and Methodist choirs. Armitage is at his best when he describes an idiosyncratic Yorkshire where the people, at least in the fantasy world of north country humour, give quaint answers to simple questions – a world in which grandma, when told of a new crown filling asks. "Why, what have you won this time?"

Perhaps the story of the filling provides part of the explanation of why *All Points North* rarely quite lives up to its first paragraph – an account of how two Yorkshire fishermen worried what all the fuss was about when they caught a mine on the end of their line. The filling was made of gold. No real Yorkshireman would waste money on such extravagance. Three years at Portsmouth Polytechnic have clearly taken their toll on Simon Armitage's standards and values.

Younger than Yesterday

by Jane Holland

DAVID HART

Setting The Poem to Words

Five Seasons Press, £8.50
ISBN 0 947960 19 8

DINAH LIVINGSTONE

May Day

Katabasis, £6.95
ISBN 0 904872 27 0

GEOFFREY HOLLOWAY

And Why Not?
Selected Poems 1972-1994

Flambard, £7.99
ISBN 1 873226 20 9

EVANGELINE PATERSON

A Game Of Soldiers

Stride, £6.95
ISBN 1 900152 21 5

IAN CAWS

Herrick's Women

University of Salzburg, £4.95
ISBN 3 7052 0972 8

IF INITIATION IS the gateway to the first collection, reinitiation is that breathlessly elusive act of recognition necessary before further poetry can be realised. Sadly, few poets satisfactorily achieve reinitiation once they are, to borrow Dante's famous phrase, "*nel mezzo del cammin di nostra vita*". It's not that poetry is essentially bound up with youth but rather that it requires innocence, faith and boundless optimism, none of them qualities readily associated with middle age. In that dark forest, you have to be able to see the wood for the trees. Human nature being largely immune to such concerns, however, most people carry on writing and publishing long after the blessing of initiation has passed. And when I say that most of these poets, though all experienced hands, are not better known because they do not deserve to be better known, am I criticising the work itself or simply their continuing desire to be heard?

But value judgements like that assume that there is a "right" way to be a poet, a particular way of writing that most people recognise as being mainstream, and these poets, with the possible exception of David Hart, will never be shoehorned into our tightly regulated criteria. To be given such work to review in a magazine as irretrievably mainstream as *Poetry Review* is to ask questions of these poets which may not apply to them. But in asking them, interesting conflicts within the poetry world must necessarily be highlighted and examined, and if the end result is to move the goal posts slightly, something important will surely have been achieved.

David Hart
David Hart's concentrated vision, in *Setting the Poem to Words*, is one which deserves to be recognized and widely-read, not simply because he has talent but because he takes risks. It seems to me that risk-taking is the area in which these other poets fall short, and although form is a big part of that, I also mean other risks taken within the poems: structural, linguistic, syntactical. The other poets in this selection have an enormous respect for poetry, and too much respect hampers personal development. I applaud anyone who can place their tongue so firmly in their cheek as to open a poem with: "A pure white iguana has entered the pure white room / and the name of the iguana is *iguana, purest white*" ('Pure white iguana').

He's also unafraid to switch sides. "Nobody ever gets beaten up in my poems / or cuts their own wrists / or dies in a car crash" is an example of his take on loose-limbed American post-modernism,

yet in a flash he's comically and irreverently elliptic: "knees up // o // Brum bard // above the drone" ('Poem', subtitled 'For Roy Fisher In The Year Of His 65th Birthday'). An unwillingness to experiment is one of the traits I find most frustrating in contemporary British poets, yet it's almost endemic. Perhaps people equate diversity with a lack of focus, wrongly in my opinion. I'm not talking about experimentation for its own sake, but rather a desire, based on total understanding of form, to push language to its limits, see what it can do under pressure. David Hart's work is a good example of that desire.

Dinah Livingstone
By contrast, Dinah Livingstone is a poet to whom such concerns seem unimportant. In 'May Day', she wants to explain, to persuade, not to play about with an intractable medium. Her understanding of the line-break may be unerringly accurate, but she is too content with mediocrity to exploit that talent.

I don't think Livingstone's work is essentially bad (although lines like "I try to avoid the rabbit droppings" make my jaw drop, possibly due to an overdeveloped sense of aesthetics) and her purpose certainly benefits from an evenness of tone, but I knew we had little in common on reading the deathless back-cover blurb: "both country and city poems are full of birds and trees". Nothing wrong in that. Our Poet Laureate built his reputation on such things. And indeed, there are birds and trees galore, but not a single Hughesian signpost in sight. I am aware of her many previous collections. I appreciate the quiet confidence behind her loosely iambic structure. But I am unconvinced that anyone who can end a poem with: "Swishing numinous trees be my archangels" can have anything useful to add to twentieth-century poetry. And that, which probably sounds like a thoughtless insult, is actually a point of tremendous importance. At their best, these backwaters may be picturesque, but they are too vague to push us into the next century.

Geoffrey Holloway
So what am I saying? That it should be all hands on deck as we pass the millennium? I believe so. This is no time for Georgianesque reminiscences. Which leads me neatly to Geoffrey Holloway, who died last year, and with whom I had some contact through my magazine, *Blade. And Why Not?* is a

selection of his best work from 1972–1994. Holloway was born in 1918, when T. S. Eliot and Pound had already swept away the aimless conventionality of the Georgians, and that awareness of daring permeates his work without the more recent misinterpretation of "anything goes". In 'The Sign', he describes the moment of initiation, "the thing never to be told", perfectly:

> And no whisper, no backwards incantation
> can swerve it ever
> from its crucial instant –
> arriving charged with sensuous adoration,
> the radiant destiny of tribute,
> to gain, grace, pass on.

Now this is poetry I can rejoice in. But the fact that Holloway hovered just outside the mainstream throughout his career points less to clique mentality and more to his inability to maintain that standard consistently. He was always being drawn aside, back into the cosy world of poetry magazines and occasional verse, and no doubt that was right from his point of view. In 'Dusk', he looks back over his shoulder, more with resignation than regret: "I am following a man who remembers me / only in snatches // . ..I am following a man with a key sewn into a glove / he has lost". To steal from E. M. Forster, Geoffrey Holloway was a poet who could "see life steadily and see it whole", and it's right to pay tribute to that ability, whilst wishing perhaps that the mainstream had been a little wider, if only in order to include him at his best.

Evangeline Paterson

Evangeline Paterson is another poet whose standard of work is inconsistent. The title poem is an appalling re-take of 'The Grand Old Duke of York', which ends:

> Oh the grand old Duke of York
> he had a wooden head
> but he'll still be marching round and round
> when the rest of us are dead.

There is also a strain of the Alan Bennetts in Paterson's short narrative lyrics, complete with old ladies, handicapped loved ones, and deathless concluding lines like: "Her husband, in his slippers, brings her tea". Accessible, yes, but dreary with it.

Yet Paterson clearly has depths beyond the purely anecdotal – connected, I suspect, to her Irish

roots. In 'A Game of Soldiers', she occasionally produces something original out of an experimental urge: "Old sorceress, dream-haunter / I have slipped your noose // I am out into air // ... – a ruckle of bones / hirpling on my track" ('Crone'). But ironically the majority of these poems are summed up, by Paterson herself, in the concluding lines of this collection: "never could make no music / out of your words".

Ian Caws

Ian Caws, in his Preface to *Herrick's Women*, makes the point that "A book, like a poem, should be more than the sum of its parts". This is a dictum close to my own heart, and certainly Caws has achieved an overall unity with this latest collection. His formal qualities mark him out from the other poets here. Although never interested in abandoning form, his poems play freely within their chosen metres and rhyme schemes. They involve themselves with an everyday reality without becoming trite or painful to read. In 'Privacy', Caws explains his motivation:

> "Why do you write?" she asked,
> Looking across green wheatfields to the downs.
> "Because", I said, "between pen and paper
> Is the last privacy."

Liking Herrick's work myself, I was eager to read this collection, but still couldn't bring myself to empathise with someone whose response to life is so formalised. I don't think my desire for free verse is a question of being unable to "understand" form, since I was brought up on rhyme and metre. It's more that I find a strict adherence to form inadequate as an expression of modern life. It binds the English language in a way that seems acceptable, even necessary, in Shakespeare or the Metaphysicals, but which doesn't allow, as Evangeline Paterson sensed, that sensuous music to emerge which is more natural for our age. But Caws provides the right note to end a review which took Dante as a starting-point, as another not-so-young poet continually attempting to achieve reinitiation, demonstrated here in 'Rainbows':

> And perhaps what I have always stopped for,
> Though distracted by sloth or fantasy,
> Was that second rainbow which climbed too far
> And appeared only once, that nobody
> Acknowledged or offered intimacy.

From the Pamphlet Pile

by Matt Holland

HERE IS A question that might baffle many well-read quiz panelists but not, one supposes, most *PR* readers. What, in the world of books, are the following? Slow Dancer, Crabflower, Flarestack, Jackson's Arm, Mudfog, Waldean, Redbeck, Shoestring, Tabla, Akros, Clarion, Corridor, Scratch, Rack, Dagger, and Dog.

So, now that we know who publishes the pamphlets, another obvious question must be, who do they serve? One acceptable if uninformed answer might be, the poet, the printer, and the passionate few readers, the latter being that very important if tiny minority who know that good writing does not always or immediately find big publishers and possibly never big readership. These are the seekers who dare to recognise and delight in "language charged with meaning" wherever they find it. Recently, witnessing one pioneering poet, Sarah-Jane Arbury, put together a photocopied and stapled anthology of new writers, the result of a weeklong workshop with children and adults down on a ramshackle old farm, and seeing it sell like hot cakes and be read with delight, reminded this reviewer of the real need to create with words and then the real thrill of "publishing" the results, affirming and immortalising your work. When you see this process happening first hand, judgement of poets' motives and even poetic standards, is set aside, at least for a while.

But when you are faced with a pile of properly bound A5 booklets, sombre-looking publications on Italian Rivoli or French Canson paper, in limited editions, "50 copies reserved for the collaborators", which describe the author as "deeply important", you can't help but ask an awkward question, or three, and know that others will too. And you are unlikely to be satisfied with the answer that there is a long tradition in the printing of pamphlets and "fine books". In an attempt to overcome your uncertainties you decide that it might be more useful to try to forget the packaging and go on simply to look at the poems, let them do the talk-ing, and hope they yield some answers.

Roger McGough's *Pen Pals*, from Prospero Poets (unpriced), with lots of loose illustrations in it by Annie long-biog Newnham, is a pamphlet full of one single poem that ends with a letter-bomb. It is a clever prosy little piece about a wife's affair with a postman but you can't help wondering if, as a poem, it merits the thick paper, the blank pages, and all those editor and designer credits. Precious, cool, or what? Not at all McGough, you'd have thought. But this seems to be the Prospero house style. They do the same for Matthew Sweeney's *Blue Taps* (unpriced), printed on English Palazzo Castile Ivory and American Gainsborough Camel, no less, but at least we get three memorable poems, one beginning thus: "A shoelace and a penis lying in a field / on a cold, blue, February morning".

Talking of laces, Shoestring heed the Prospero call and go for thick covers but do their own thing inside with lots of pages of ordinary paper with loads of poems on them. Roger Green's *Wolvercote Dreaming* (£2.95) is a good and substantial read, part Oxonian and parochial, part anthropological and global, but all the while literary *in extremis*, especially in its myriad allusions. Maurice Rutherford's *After the Parade* (£2.95) is equal in content volume, a couple of dozen pages with poems on most of them, and is also homely but in a less detached way, with greater use of the vernacular and the ready-made phrase. This makes you wonder what editorial policy Shoestring employs. At Redbeck they appear to have consistent standards both in packaging and poetry. In Clare Crossman's *Landscapes* (£3.75) and Howard Wright's *Usquebaugh* (£3.95) most of the poems have a strong contemporary style and tone, are challenging in ideas and yet consistently accessible without being too full of feelings easily let loose.

Easy to handle, and even to pocket, are the little Smith/Doorstop collections. Terrific value at £2.95, with just the right amount of biographical detail, and packed with poems to read, wherever you are. Michael Laskey (*In a Fruit Cage*), Jonathan Davidson (*A Horse Called House*), Jane Draycott (*No Theatre*), and Andrew Wilson (*Des for Pres*) (who dares to start a poem like this: "Then there were the chickens"), are a particularly strong quartet on their list.

Doubtless the strength of the poets determines what financial help is given to small presses by regional arts boards. And maybe it is the strength of literature development workers that gets libraries involved too. In Hereford and Worcester they've certainly shown sound judgement in supporting Flarestack's publication of Miriam Obrey's *A Case for More Heads* and Charles Johnson's *A Box of Professional Secrets*, who both have the courage to look at country life in a way that *Country Life* does not. Obrey tells it like this: "Forget the house cow at the orchard gate, / village choirs and WI – / yesterday my father arrived / his teeth kicked in by a racehorse – / his eye blacked by the husband of his latest lay".

There are plenty of pamphlet poets whose work merits attention but who appear not to get any financial help in being published. Doubtless it was ever thus. But Jackson's Arm/Sunk Island, and Dog publications, who give us Amanda Dalton's *Room of Leaves* and Peter Lewin's *Knightwood*, both of which are top-heavy with that big personal pronoun "I", may be providing a therapy as well as a poetry

service. Perhaps they are one and the same; and you and I are doing it too, maybe. And ministering to our need is pamphlet poetry.

Addresses of the Presses

Prospero Poets, Clarion Press, Neatham Mill, Holybourne, Alton, Hampshire GU34 4NP

Shoestring Press, 19 Devonshire Avenue, Beeston, Nottingham, NG9 1BS

Redbeck Press, 24 Aireville Road, Frizinghall, Bradford BD9 4HH

Smith/Doorstop Books, The Poetry Business, The Studio Byram Arcade' Huddersfield HD1 1ND

Flarestack Publishing, Reditch Library, 15 Market Place, Redditch, Worcestershire B98 8AR

Jackson's Arm, Sunk Island Publishing, PO Box 74, Lincoln LN1 1QG

DOG, 32B Breakspears Road, London SE4 1UW

Stampersations

by Ian McMillan

Binary Myths

Edited by Andy Brown
Stride Publications, £ 6.95
ISBN 1 90015245 2

IN A RECENT editorial in *The North*, Peter Sansom wrote that when he picked up a poetry magazine he always read the prose first: the biographical notes, the reviews, the articles. Well, I'm with Peter on that one, and maybe that's why I like *Binary Myths* so much. It's subtitled "Conversations with Contemporary Poets", although they're really stampersations as they're interviews conducted by post about each particular poet's view of language and the way we use it.

One good thing about the book is that the poets aren't The Usual Suspects. In fact they're mainly The Unusual Suspects: writers like Miles Champion, Sheila E. Murphy and cris cheek rub shoulders with more media-haggard names like David Kennedy and Sarah Maguire. The questions, it has to be said, are on the po-faced axis of serious,

but the answers are often lively and thought-provoking, and very cheering about the Present State of Poetry. cris cheek is the liveliest respondent, as you'd expect. His enthusiasm is contagious, bursting out of Slim Volume Avenue into a hardly-mapped heaven of wide inviting streets. When asked what he's reading now, he replies "poetics, graphic novels, essays, newspapers, magazines, blurbs, advertising slogans, performance texts, text-based installations, packaging, car number plates (you translate the numbers into letters)", and when asked about what interests him in contemporary poetry he launches into a splendid riff that I can only quote from, but which includes "Orality re-ascendant. Spoken word in performance...proliferations of dialect writing...non standard spellings". Are you listening, Mr. Blunkett?

What's fascinating throughout the interviews is the way that different poets have answered similar questions. Miles Champion is reading an entire Reading List, including Barret Watten, Walter Benjamin and Clark Coolidge in amongst loads of writers I've not read and some I've not heard of; David Kennedy is reading a completely different gang, including John Ash and Deryn Rees-Jones, and Eva Salzman is on with Pat Barker, Dee Brown's *Bury My Heart at Wounded Knee* and Vikram Seth. I'm cheering here for two reasons. First because hardly any names crop up twice, and second because my own haphazard and impulsive reading is somehow vindicated by this plurality. I used to feel guilty because I wasn't following some kind of taste-oriented Literature Course. I don't now.

As an inveterate collaborator, I was interested to read the poets' answers to the question "Have you collaborated with any other writers or artists recently?", and again the range is refreshing and somehow life (or at least art) affirming. John Bumside is working with visual artists; cris cheek is continuing to work with dance and visual art; David Kennedy is working with Christopher Pilling on translations of surrrealist poetry, and so on. The overall feeling is one of vast activity and a huge willingness to engage with others to create new work, and on a personal level I feel empowered, having read this book, to continue with my own collaborations with visual artists, musicians, and theatre practicioners.

I'll have to mention Eva Salzman's rant (her description) because it's so powerful: it's a smack in the face of The Literary Life and the reputation-makers and the establishmenteers. Her feelings towards one particular poet come to surface here very strongly and widen into a discussion of gender and power and reputation that should perhaps be required reading for anyone doing Creative Writing at college and is thinking about a literary career.

There are a couple of things I don't like about the book; one is that it looks so bloody dull that hardly anyone would guess, just by looking at it, what lustrous gems lie within, and the other is the title. It sounds like a Phd or the name of a band from late 1975. In fact I think I saw them supporting Gentle Giant. Ignore the way the book looks, ignore the title (call it "Stampersations with the Unusual Suspects" if you like). Just buy it, read it and enjoy it. Now, please welcome on stage The Binary Myths playing the whole of their new Concept Album...

Safe Pair of Hands

by Peter Forbes

SIMON RAE

Rapid Response
Poems from the Guardian 1991–1996

Headland, £6.95
ISBN 0 903074 96 6

SIMON RAE HAS inherited the mantle of Roger Woddis, the safe pair of hands with any contemporary topic, to be delivered in the most appropriate verse form. Topical poets, like cartoonists, to whom they are closely related, set up a typical rounded human figure – pleasure-loving, commonsensical, no better than they ought to be and roll the world's doings past them to show how outrageously far they depart from anything they are likely to approve of.

In his introduction Simon Rae says that the later poems draw on personal experience more often than the early ones do ("Sniping at a corrupt and corrupting government week after week can get wearisome"). In this he is in line with the general tendency of the press to prefer columnists' views to news, although a poet has a good deal more excuse.

The topical poet gets the chance to pastiche his or her favourite poems and Rae does Auden's 'Tell me the Truth About Love', 'Naming of Parts', 'This be the Verse' ("They tuck you up your Mum and Dad"), 'Cargoes', 'The Rolling English Road', 'A Subaltern's Love Song', and 'If', among others. His verse is always efficient at least and can get up a fair head of steam given the right subject and form:

> Is its manner at parties Abrasive?
> Does it loom with terrified smile?
> Are its answers to questions evasive?
> Are its speeches a horrible trial?
> Does it often succumb to distractions?
> Does it think the electorate a shower?
> Just what are its greatest attractions?
> Oh tell me the truth about power.
> ('Tell Me The Truth About Power')

Rae is at his best on things he cares about personally, sport for example. 'Ode on a Goal' (also included in Wendy Cope's The Funny Side), a tribute to Paul Gascoigne, is reminiscent of Gavin Ewart at his best: "savour simply the sublime control / Like angels performing rock'n'roll / On the dance-floor of a pinhead. Extol / That goal!"

My My My My Generation

JAMES KEERY ON GLYN MAXWELL'S FORAY INTO ENGLISH PASTORAL

GLYN MAXWELL

The Breakage

Faber, £7.99
ISBN 0 571 19337 4

GLYN MAXWELL'S CONTRIBUTION to the 'Songlines' issue of *Poetry Review* was a manifesto on behalf of "the first generation of poets to have been significantly and unashamedly affected by the best days of rock music ... As the axeman says, let's do it". Go, Glyn! It's true that he fluffed it a bit by conceding that a Dylan lyric is "doggerel" on the page, which is like sneering at a black-and-white illustration of a painting. On 'Don't Look Back', a John Lee Hooker track recorded in his Them days, Van Morrison makes two words, "Stop dreaming", last forever. Still, I found the attack on "contemporary poets who look down their noses at the people who wrote 'Imagine' [and] 'Forever Young'"a wonderfully heartening one.

Disarming, too, but, happily for the task in hand, Maxwell's smack at reviewers – "Don't waste your time on telling me / My purpose, point or pedigree" – had a pleasantly restorative effect. Precursors include Auden, Paul Muldoon and the hungry hobo ("If I had some ham, I'd have me some ham 'n' eggs ... if I had some eggs..."). The first of his poems I came across was the uncollected 'Angel and Caroline' (*PN Review* #55, 1987): "angels // never cease to amaze and solidly, baldly, / they believe like girls. / Then leap up bare / and say they'll make the coffee! Then, // they patter away like rain...". It's an anthology of the tricksy niceties

> I prefer the brashness of "the Mayor's son" ("I could define Elizabeth. I will: / Every girl you ever wanted, but / can't have 'cause I want"), so it came as a surprise to discover that "all those characters have decamped *en masse* towards a darkened theatre where they wait to be auditioned for the verse-plays to which I mean to devote the years to come".
>
> It isn't that I shall miss "the crimson team" or the Manzadinka-drinker, but I'm not at all sure about the "quieter, briefer voice that speaks ... about things quite personal to me, even things that actually happened".

of early O'Hara and just hits off his deadpan lilt (compare 'The Muse Considered as a Demon Lover': "oh I'd never let that angel // go! But seriously it said to me 'I've / got to get a bun'. My feet went blind"). It's fitting that it appeared next to 'A Christening', an Ash(bery) poem by Peter Sansom ("Too bad, then, for the people in the unwritten / chapters..."), influences transmitted, via the Poetry Business workshop, to Simon Armitage, whose first collection, *Zoom!*, contains the obligatory Huddersfield cover of O'Hara's 'Poem' by way of response to Geoff Hattersley's 'Simon's Book' (*Slouching Towards Rotherham*, 1987): "I thought / about old what's-his-name picking up / Simon's book and getting none of it". These excellent poets are Maxwell's generation: Faber got it right in casting him alongside Armitage in the remake of *Letters from Iceland*.

Armitage has the better of *Moon Country*, but it's Maxwell who has taken Auden on at his own game. The celebrated 'Helene and Heloise', fifteen rhyming sixains in which the poet, "inscrutable" in sunglasses, considers two blonde girls as they swim "in the embassy pool", blends 'A Summer Night' ("the sexy airs of summer, / The bathing hours and the bare arms") with 'The Shield of Achilles': "That girls were raped, that two boys knife a third, / Were axioms to him...". The contrast between what Thetis expects to see on the shield and what Hephaestos "had put instead" is devastating, but Maxwell seems to think that the proximity of "a squad / Of infuriated coldly eyeing sons / Kicking the screaming oath out of anyone's" qualifies him to patronise the poor little rich "breathtakers" something rotten:

Still, I'd think of Helene, of Heloise
Moving harmless, shieldless into a dull
And dangerous hot breeze,
With nothing but hopes to please, delight, fulfil
Some male as desperate and foul as this is,
Who'd not hurt them for all their limited kisses.

I prefer the insouciance of "the brown-haired bloke" in 'Tale of a Chocolate Egg', even the brashness of "the Mayor's son" in his "stylish trilby hat" ("I could define Elizabeth. I will: / Every girl you ever wanted, but / can't have 'cause I want"), so it came as a surprise to discover that "all those characters have decamped *en masse* towards a darkened theatre where they wait to be auditioned for the verse-plays to which I mean to devote the years to come". It isn't that I shall miss "Robbing Wood", "the crimson team" or the Manzadinka-drinker, but I'm not at all sure about the "quieter, briefer voice that speaks ... about things quite personal to me, even things that actually happened". Maxwell made these remarks some years ago, but they apply less to *Rest for the Wicked*, of which the highlight is 'Phaeton and the Chariot of the Sun', starring equine equivalents of Phil, Meg and Herk the Jerk, than to *The Breakage*, in which "a deep concern for England" (blurb) manifests itself in a whole series of rewrites of Larkin's 'MCMXIV'. 'My Grandfather at the Pool' elegizes the sole survivor of the trenches among the five young men in the sepia cover photo; in 'An August Monday', the dispenser of malicious awards "for services / To ruining my day" snaps out of his early Maxwell poem to find himself under shellfire; 'Valentines at the Front' closes with a dewy-eyed vision of "untold villages of untold brides"; and so on. "Never such innocence again". Cue Eleanor Farjeon:

Dear Edward, just a note to say we're here
And nowhere could be better. And your key
Was where you said it would be, and the air
Is fresh with things you think...

Anything less like 'Letter to Lord Byron' would be hard to imagine. The fourteen 'Letters to Edward Thomas' are rich in layered poignancies, such as that allusion to 'Digging' ("Today I think / Only with scents") and the unelucidated reference to "Robert's *North of Boston* in your kit", which "They gave to me, not needing it": Thomas had been reviewing for two papers, giving Farjeon his second review copy. *Edward Thomas: The Last Four Years* is

an engaging memoir of house-parties, "word games Adam taught to Eve, and some / Eve knew but never told him", merry exploits ("Nut after nut succumbed to Bertie's deadliest yorkers") and deepening devotion to the poet. The author of 'Morning Has Broken' might have enjoyed some of her lines: "To see grey dawn arrive and blush to find us / Watching, late enchanted into early". The subtle lushness of that personification is exactly what Farjeon responded to in Thomas's prose: "Had she leaped out of the earth or out of the sky to express in human shape the loveliness of the hour, she could not have been made otherwise by a sculptor god...". For her, this is "the key to one of Edward's dreams" – no wonder it took Frost to find the key to his poetry. Farjeon may gush, but neither pompous bathos ("Edward Thomas, great / Unknowable, omniscient, your cottage / Waits for you...") nor affectation ("And reason not my need, / Who writes what nobody but she will read") is her style at all.

The last letter is in the new voice of the poet himself: "Dear Edward Thomas, Frost died, I was born...". Maxwell intimates that he is "writing this at dawn, / Where Robert lived, in Amherst", where he now teaches. For so deeply loved he England... but it's not his enthusiastic exile that troubles me so much as his belletristic Georgian pathos. I wouldn't mind, but the sequence is dedicated to the same Derek Walcott whose surly insistence that "the rock stars are doing your work" got Maxwell going!

The finest poem in *The Breakage* crystallizes my reservations. 'Edward Wilson' is an elegy for one of the casualties of Scott's expedition:

...A late English saint
has only eggs to save, himself to warm,

picturing Oriana. Lost winds
tug at the sketchbook. Shaded round, the eyes
Scott has to look at till tomorrow ends
are unenquiring and as blue as skies.

There is admirable economy in the way the name of Wilson's wife is allowed to hint at Elizabethan glory and in the allusions to the Emperor Penguin's eggs, imperial trophies of a previous near-fatal expedition, and Scott's last letter: "His eyes have a comfortable blue look of hope". Pathos, courage and faith are there for the taking, with the stiff-upper-lip wetness of Andrew Motion. Then again, for all I know, you may *like* Andrew Motion.

Bit Parts in the Epic

by John Greening

GEORGE SZIRTES

**Portrait of My Father
in an English Landscape**

Oxford Poets, £7.99

ISBN 0 19288091 8

THIS BOOK IS about the need to keep on creating in the face of chaos, and it is certainly a showcase of George Szirtes' own skills as a formal craftsman. 'The First, Second, Third and Fourth Circles' is characteristic: a portrait of city life as viewed from Budapest's ring-roads. Szirtes the artist (and there are many poems here about art) likes to frame things, enjoys the tension between encircling roads and the restless, stifling confinement of existence within. There are, of course, shades of Dante, too:

Nineteenth-century grid-maps where everyone lives
but wants to move out of, in one room or two rooms
or one and a half-rooms, ranged about the
communal courtyard,
the sound of a tap or a radio, a beggar or busker,
under the residents' own square of sky...

It is obsessive, like graffiti scrawled on concrete, but it works, weaving its own grave music. Szirtes takes Wallace Stevens' "idea of order" and finds it as elusive on the Attila József Estate as it was at Key West. Art takes its place as a still point in this turning world, yet 'Golden Bream', for example, shows that there is a rush-hour of decomposition behind the most formal of compositions:

It may be nature morte *but it's still life*, said the joky
sixties poet
and I'm sure he is right, because there is death in it,
not just in the codified clutter of skulls, books and
bubbles
but in the whole enterprise and so particularly
when plainly dead creatures, like pheasants and
hares,
quails, sparrows, orioles and trout (but chiefly the
birds)
do so much lolloping and hanging, neatly
shimmered up,

displayed with the instrument of their final bringing
down,
and garnished with a few tasteful etceteras such as
flowers...

Elsewhere there is a familiar Szirtesian taste for dark whimsy. The opening piece, 'Rabbits' (another addition to that curious treasury of post-war British rabbit poems!) conjures up more than furriness, more even than myxomatosis: "Something of terror remains in the grass / where the rabbits have been...". These vulnerable, nameless, huddled masses, who disappear as a train passes are like refugees or Holocaust victims.

My favourite poem in this book is one of the 'Four Villonesques on Desire', about Obsessives, but the most remarkable achievement is the title poem, 'Portrait of my Father in an English Landscape', the last of a series of *three* Hungarian Sonnet sequences. *Sonnets redoublé*, or double crowns of sonnets have become rather fashionable (I recently recommended Tessa Rose Chester's in these pages): fourteen sonnets, sharing first and last lines, which are then redeployed in order as the lines of a fifteenth. This form is tricky enough to try once, but to publish three must be unique. Szirtes pulls it off (albeit with a little rule-bending) and one can see why the form – as well as its Hungarian provenance – appeals to him, It is a high-wire act and there is a touch of the drum-roll, a sense of effort, of proud and deliberate artifice ("the figure I feel I have to build / into and out of language"); but he conceives of life as at once epic and fragmented, which is exactly the feeling this verse form evokes: "things being just as they are, true without consequence, bit parts / in a ridiculous epic of cinematic dust".

Szirtes uses "pre-ordained" formal difficulties to confront the challenge of coherency, which is a topic that obsesses him – unsurprisingly for one brought out of Revolution to live in a foreign country at the age of eight. His poems fight their own tendency to drift away from their apparent subjects. This drifting sometimes becomes the subject, as in 'Mouth Music', with its refrain, "said the dying man...", justification enough for some very bizarre cataloguing. There is occasionally the feeling with Szirtes' rhymes that his taste for the surreal leaves too many choices open – the more improbable the better: "Grandad got run down by a tram / and yet survived to claim the insurance. One / uncle opened a music shop. It closed like a clam / about him". Do we say that's a startlingly original simile or – with Ben Jonson – that he is "wresting words from their true calling; / propping verse for fear of falling"? His poems are like good studies (they remind me of some Hungarian violin pieces I couldn't play): they do not merely exercise their forms, they are driven by them. In the painterly sense, they are studies of human nature, pages of a sketch-pad scattered with sharp, intense images, attempts to get something right, preparatory rather than conclusive.

An Heroic Shrug

by Adam Thorpe

DAVID HARSENT

A Bird's Idea of Flight

Faber £7.99

ISBN 0 571 19329 3

THERE WAS A brief fashion in the seventeenth century for poems in the form of dialogues between Charon, the ferryman of the Styx, and a living mortal desperate to bring back a lost loved one. These dialogues served as contemporary commentaries, full of up-to-date allusions and risqué jokes; despite the emotional and philosophical persuasions of the lover, Charon was never outwitted, rough as he was. The authority of Hades reared behind him, and it was just that dread certainty that the poets liked to fling their words against.

Something of the atmosphere of these dialogues wreathes about David Harsent's impressive descent into Death's realms, balancing Dante's loftier presence. It's a dream journey flickered through by the trickster image of the hare (a symbol of the borderline between the conscious and unconscious), and a pop-eyed "bundle of bones" straight out of a fourteenth-century fresco. It begins, fittingly for a densely referential work thick with "jiggery-pokery and waterworn scholia", in an archivist's vellum-creaking study. Armed only with a wasted life and a notebook, the poet sets out to learn about death, particularly his own. But the cryptic archivist is the first of many disappointments: executioners, prostitutes, drunks, dancing catacomb attendants and jaundiced friends like Blind Harry – a cast out of nightmare or fever attend these vivid wanderings, and leave both the poet and reader equally bemused by their oracular advice and caustic insights.

This morbid odyssey is quick with life. The imagery is darting rather than confusing, fired by a snappy yet sensual language, the lines bobbing hypnagogically just where poetry brews itself most potently. As in dream, images repeat themselves, shift their frames, elongate and enclose; in perhaps my favourite poem, 'The Locket', the poet wakes up and finds himself in a whacky night-time beach-party which had previously appeared only as a simile. He sleeps with a girl and finds himself imprinted with her "ragged splash / of a strawberry-mark that went by the point of her jaw / to her throat and down the dip / of her collarbone, like a blush or the start of spoilage in fruit". Death and the maiden in the age of AIDS, perhaps.

Harsent is a mean wielder of free verse, but the bass-line is anapaestic, and he can keep a run-on clause going for two pages. These wild and lengthy riffs may strike some tastes as monotonous, and certainly the plangent note is missing, despite the subject. But plangency has little place in what is really an obsessive's hunt for information on something which we can anatomise and elegise, but never elucidate. At least not beyond a certain point marked Faith. The poet studies the drowned (sailors frozen to death in the rigging are like "birds in a leafless tree"), and the dusty inhabitants of the catacombs – "Over here were the famous twins, got up / in broderie-anglaise caps / and party frocks, still holding hands" – but he isn't really getting what he wants.

What is it he wants? On a lonely beach, sunning himself by a whinbush, he tells the tick-riddled hare that it's

> Something... as much a nugget
> as a bird's idea of flight.

This haunting line (see the book's title and dropped-feather cover) is affirmed by the laughing hare: "That's what it is... that's just / what you'll come to, dreamless and changeless, / alone in some place like this, or one in a crowd". As close as we come to an answer, then; perhaps the most striking image in the sequence is that of a bird beating against the rose window of a buried cathedral, chiming with the various instances of birds in cages, suffocated birds, a bird drumming its wings against an anatomist's pane. But nothing nudges us closer to the other side of the rose window, to what we imagine might lie on the other side, than poetry that lies cheek-by-jowl with dream. No wonder castaways are allowed Shakespeare and the Bible.

The irony, Harsent seems to be pointing out, is that death is the end of dream. The flickering activity of the brain, the dank depths and dark streets and mossy smiles of its continual reassembling, is exactly what shuts down when the plugs are pulled "on the hubbub of dungeony / SFX". Or, as the tattooed companion of his dreams puts it, clutching the vodka:

> when someone you claim to recognise climbs up
> out of your bones
> and legs it for the door
> without so much as a kiss
> my-arse-goodbye...

If there's an implied shrug at the end of Harsent's endeavour, at least we sense its heroism: and a heroic shrug is about right, at the end of this particular millennium.

Pleasures of the Closed Door

by Kwame Dawes

LUCILLE CLIFTON

Terrible Stories

Slow Dancer Poetry, £6.99
ISBN 1 871033 42 X

BEVERLIEY BRAUNE

Camouflage

Bloodaxe Books, £6.95
ISBN 1 85224 271 X

MIMI KHALVATI

Entries on Light

Carcanet, £6.95p
ISBN 1 85754 329 7

LUCILLE CLIFTON'S *TERRIBLE Stories* (first published in 1996 in the USA) contain stories of reflection, reflection on the unresolved and perhaps eternally enigmatic themes of her experience. She offers few answers but is quite aware that her verse will constantly ask questions in that direct, carefully honed style of hers that at times achieves the elegance of a well-executed line drawing – efficient and profoundly moving. Clifton understands irony – indeed it is irony that shores up these poems, that

gives them their music and their distinction. This collection's themes can be listed – indeed she offers the list in one of her poems – an untitled piece that opens the section 'In the Mean Time':

> evening and my dead once husband
> rises up from the spirit board
> through the trembled air i moan
> the names of our wayward sons
> and ask him to explain why
> i fuss like a fishwife why
> cancer and terrible loneliness
> and the wars against our people
> and the room glimmers as if washed
> in tears and out of the mist a hand
> becomes flesh and i watch
> as its pointing fingers spell

I quote so much of the poem because of its remarkable usefulness as an index to the collection. The tone of the piece, a kind of mournful reflection on the enigma of mortality is carried through the entire collection. Her interest in the idea of being an "honest woman" and not a "fishwife" or a fox are caught in the first movement of the book titled 'A Dream of Foxes'. Here the fox represent what Lorna Goodison describes as the "wild woman", her dangerous alter-ego that at once seduces her and appalls her. In Clifton's version, the fox / vixen woman moves from the alter ego to the central ego – she is the good woman, and now she is transformed into a gathering of strong willed women strolling through the bush: "only a lovely line / of honest women stepping / without fear or guilt or shame / safe through the generous fields".

In the second movement of poems, Clifton writes with power and terrible grace about cancer.

The confessional quality is granted a steely confidence by Clifton's capacity to derive irony from the loneliness and fear of the moment. In '1994' she observes "how dangerous it is // to be born with breasts / you know how dangerous it is / to wear black skin". There is, in this, a wry wit that is tempered by an acute capacity to discover moments of beauty, the capacity to see beauty despite unbelief: "then rock so wonderful / you forget you have no faith" ('down the tram'). From this delicate exploration of cancer's effects, Clifton tackles her third theme, the wars against her people. Her poems do not contain predictable complaints about racism, but they constitute a review of progress or the lack thereof. There is something contemporary about her examination of racism – the enemies are now so close they seem almost harmless, yet it is in her capacity to recognize that the Black American experience is sometimes more about how Blacks contend with their personal and collective past than about what has been done to them that gives her verse such resonance. The south for her is an old fur coat bequeathed to her by her mother. Clifton is at her best with such deftly apprehended epiphanies:

> i will wear it
> because she loved it
> but the blood from it pools
> on my shoulders
> heavy and dark and alive.
>
> ('entering the south')

Shifting from the pained observations of a woman who understands that she is getting older and that she is still trying to find meaning in her world, the collection ends with a series of poems that retell segments of the life of David and, in the process, become intimations on faith and legacy in a world of constant temptations and hardships. The finger on the wall, however, does not promise spiritual comfort and assurance to Clifton – instead, she finds beauty in the humanity of David, in his capacity to fail. Her David ages with questions deep in him: "how can this david love himself. / be loved (i am singing and spinning now) / if he stands in the tents of history / bloody skull in one hand, harp in the other?" This is the last poem – there are no answers. There are moments when there seems to be something too normal, too unremarkable about her lines, but such moments are redeemed by the clarity of her project and the moments of elegance that litter this collection of verse.

Mimi Khalvati

Mimi Khalvati's *Entries on Light* offers a quite different formal challenge for the reader for thematically she has embarked on a daunting task, to explore through poetry that is best described as lyrical imagism, the "bearable lightness of being". *Entries* is not a long poem although the blurb on the back of the collection suggests it is. If it is a long poem it is a better seen in musical terms: variations on a theme as some symphonies are; variations not constrained by any narrative of consistent architecture that leaps off the page. There is no narrative, but a series of reflections that are conceived around the trope of the diary entry. Yet these are intimate entries, reflections of love, love-making, aging, the complex relationship between mother and daughter, the meaning of art, the meaning of exile, and so on. Diary entries allow Khalvati to roam freely for moment to moment with only a persistent preoccupation with the elements of light to ground her journeys.

The effect is at once illuminating and yet formally overwhelming. Formally so because Khalvati, while varying line lengths and the range of her assonance, remains quite committed to the iambic foot, and she avoids the mental breathing space that comes with the convention of titles by foregoing titles altogether. One then feels the compulsion to read the full collection at one sitting; a task that has its benefits, for each movement seems to demand the anchoring of the next to give it a kind of ballast, a kind of weightiness of significance. Yet at the end of the day, one is most impressed by those pieces that seem to stand best on their own, by those singular moments of epiphany that reveal the poetic imagination and that display something we have grown to admire about contemporary poets – the capacity to find extraordinary human experience inn the most ordinary of moments. This is Khalvati's manifesto, really:

> And that's
> a difference between art and nature -
> art transforming – voices, traffic
> tawdriness – but in a gathering-in
> an almost selfish motion, nature
> extending outwards as the shore its arms
> night its stars, an open invitation

Her lyric is sometimes painfully confessional and revealing, but she has the ability to find the sublime in art, the capacity to transform things into something that seems lasting. Sometimes she is so quotable: "Light comes between us and our grief / flushes it out with gold". There are so many more such gems. Yet, Khalvati finds a way of grounding the collection in a philosophical rationality that, ultimately, justifies the collection. She ends the collection with a brilliant articulation of the value of light – single moments of light in the face of encroaching darkness.

What deaths of ego, cynicism
   cowardice must we undergo
clinging to these darknesses
   we feed like ravenous mouths
forego, to unveil the simple
   moment, that open hand
on ours, both fingering back
   the curtain to reveal
a single ray?

Khalvati is not convinced by verse that seems to heavily grounded in material concerns, in the narratives of temporal time – for her, it seems, a poem must transcend the mundane, the temporal. For her politics are contained in the freedom to reflect and to sing of such reflections. There is something comforting in this even if one is always aware that the darknesses around us are sometimes far too consuming to be offset by these deft shafts of light.

Beverliey Braune

In her new collection, *Camouflage*, Beverliey Braune achieves a similar quality of lightness and reflection as do Khalvati and, to a lesser extent, Clifton. Braune, however, has not produced a collection that is as carefully organized and consistently well-crafted as the other two books. Braune's landscape is intentionally non-specific, for her true landscape is the consciousness that engages the sentiments she encounters in life.

Camouflage is Braune's first collection of poems published outside the Caribbean and it is arranged, it would seem, around selections from some of her earlier compilations of poems. The sections are all described as containing poems from this or that body of poems. One senses, then, that while there is a discernible, if slight architecture at work in the shaping of this collection, it is in fact a selected collection that shows the varied range of Braune's interests and skills, but one that suffers from some unevenness in skill.

Braune is able to turn a phrase with skill and insight – moments of genuine wit and observation. Indeed, the most elegant of these observations are in the final section of the collection, 'Voyeur Goes A-Hunting'. She watches lovers who are entwined under a fig tree and captures the danger and fierceness of their embrace in a deft image:

In the shadows of the fig tree
They are wrapped
Like sprung tornados,
Her thighs glistening with rapid light
That split the shade,

We see the same kind of efficient verse in 'Ma Donna', a poem that sustains a strained nursery rhyme quality while suggesting a sinister and taboo-breaking exploration of sexuality:

Shall I go to find them
And will they bring me home again
With my pointed breasts
And smoothened clitoris?

There are moments in some of the earlier poems when the experiments with prose poems seems to succumb to the lure of the short story – the pedestrian cadence of prose – with some of the passages running a little too long beyond the demands of a poem. The verse in the second section 'Poinsettia Fields', however, is anchored by one of the most successful movements in the collection – a series of seven poems that trace the complexities of loneliness and relationships through surreal moments of allusion and metaphor. Braune, in this movement, shows her ability to allow a metaphor to keep opening up on itself until the resulting revelation has the quality of a fresh inevitability:

Travelling alone:
passing landscapes
greeted the train again.
They flickered
upon her allergic eye.
She rubbed it to release the flint.
But the spark that waited there
launched her upon discordances,
branded her with crisp poinsettia leaves
falling from sun-dried pots
in the corner of the empty cafe.

Aural Companion

By Jenny Joseph

Sounds Good

Edited by Christopher Reid
Faber, £7.99
ISBN 0 571 19588 1

PUBLISHERS AND BOOKSELLERS need categories and labels, and a general theme or frame on a collection of poems can illuminate unnoticed pathways into understanding the material. However, I think Faber's make a misleading distinction in following Ted Hughes' anthology of poems (which they, not he, denote as primarily concerned with imagery) with 101 poems where what matters is the sound.

Hughes' poems are chosen not for their imagery but their memorability, for learning by heart. He talks about visual images as an aide-memoire in his introduction but also, and much more trenchantly than does the editor of *Sounds Good*, of the way sense and sound are implicated in language, and how this magical fusion is reinforced and made use of by poets.

A companion to this would be poems less prone to being learnt and spoken, ones written from our by now long tradition of writing for the eye to take in the shape on the page, or where the inner ear can best take in an ambiguity, or many-toned voice, rather than limiting it to one defining vocalisation.

The effect of *Sounds Good* is further muffled by the vagueness of the editor's generalizations. Much of the foreword (called an introduction on the cover) is taken up with what reads like a bet-hedging proposal to a marketing committee. Instruction is one of the purposes but Reid doesn't want to put off hypothetical non-readers for whom he thinks the provision of real knowledge, rather than chatty opinion, spoils "pleasure". On the other hand those who know and enjoy the poems can use it as a treasure chest and they are advised to "leave the notes alone and do your own thinking if you fear your pleasure may be spoilt by them". He takes space telling readers who do read notes that his are ad hoc "jottings", stray thoughts (eg. "ebb and flow" the only words on Arnold's 'Dover Beach' as a revelation of "how sound is organized within the poem"; how Lawrence does "bang on" so in 'Bavarian Gentians'; Smart's "quasi-biblical style" with no reference to his translations and versions of the psalms which made him so conversant with a foreign language's musical patterns that he could English them as the Elizabethans did the sonnet. Stating that "I have not set out to be systematic" (for fear of being thought "pedantic") may account, together with the imprecision of his prose which he would surely not condone in poetry, for the confused impression his presentation gives, but it does not excuse it.

An anthology, useful, enjoyable and instructive, which adjectives he hopes apply to his book, could certainly be based on poems where the main concern is to forefront the sound: a selection which included some nonsense verse, poems where poets consciously experiment to isolate the semantic from the acoustic, riddles, counting games, chants children play games to, baby songs and "performance" poems. This would give the reader a varied experience on which to base a consideration whether spoken language can be pure sound (it can't). It might lead them to be interested, not so much in initiation into the "secret arts of poetry composition" (a vague unjustifiable mystification rather on the level of the newspaper headline "Scandal victim at parsonage" above a tame paragraph that gives you no facts) as in the extraordinary phenomenon of language – how the sounds that vibrate on a baby's ear come to be organized into a meaningful structure and become spoken language. We can only speak what we hear.

The poems in Reid's anthology are worth reading and listening to, and thinking about, as are those in Hughes' and many another anthology. If he really had gone into "how sound is organized within the poem", with more understanding of the indivisibility of the workings of the ear and speech this anthology might have given readers a new insight into the way to experience poetry, and quickened their appetite for it. As it is I think they may get this more, as I did, from two books I came across while reading *Sounds Good*: one the American poet and teacher John Hollander's guide to English verse, *Rhyme's Reason* (Yale University Press, 1989), the other an anthology, edited, as is *Sounds Good,* by the poetry editor of its publisher (Macmillan). This has no introduction, notes or blurb, but a poem for each day of the year; Arnold's 'Dover Beach' next to a spoonerism, Yeats to Jackie Kay, Edward Thomas, Burns, 'Kubla Khan', Lewis Carroll. A brantub of a book, it is called *Read me* (Macmillan Children's Books, £4.99). I did.

KEVIN CROSSLEY-HOLLAND
AND GOD SAID

My work! It is so beautiful
And they did not realise it.

So I made monkeys of them,
Tipped loads of morning duty over them,

Turned the knife in their sides until
Each petal of blood was unbearable.

*

I hurt because they hurt me:
They could not see me clearly.

So I put into their eyes the gauze
Of morning mist in the valleys

And a double measure of pain. Still
They cannot see me clearly.

*

Syncategorematic! How clever they think
They are. True, I will not strip them

Of my word, but they keep wrapping
Themselves in words of their own.

Thousands of beatitudes, millions
Of platitudes stand between us.

*

But sometimes the scales fall from
Their eyes. They stare at green hills,

Their swelling breasts, and indolent clouds
Stooping over them. Innocent again

Of all they perpetrate, they dream
And almost know what I intended.

*

They are not just one of my rehearsals
And each day they grieve me.

How they bleat and snort and bray
And lay one another's mates.

Nerve gas, bombs, land mines!
I was right to fix their term.

*

During their dark season trust went
Into hiding: they wrote thoughts on air

And tried out their own nightmares.
Some were needed for crocodile meat.

But I have given them generation.
A few I have ennobled to say no.

*

I have bandaged their wounds with illusions.
They think their hurt is mortal,

They believe their suffering improves them
And are convinced they can change nothing.

They say I have told them
They will live again after they die.

*

I see poets – a whole unreliable army
Of egotists, promiscuous and unstable.

I am the yeast, I am the priest,
I am the alchemist, I am the conscience . . .

Listen to them! Do they really
Think they will have the last word?

*

How they go on searching for me.
Like lovers on love's threshold

They stare until their eyes burn,
And suppose they almost see me.

As if I were hiding from them
– gargantuan, dressed in skirls of cloud.

*

Taut nipple, shocking pink stem,
Loops and ropes of indigo and flame

And scarlet blossom folding in
On itself: all this before leaf-rattle,

The mouldering and dung beetle.
The fools! I gave them eyes to see.

*

Let my children hear each speckled leaf
Sing a song no less singular

Than their own. Let them enter
Into understandings with water and earth

And each unblinking stone.
Are these not ways back to me?

*

They are so powerless, so afraid
Of knocking night. Look how they sow

Seeds of stammering light
Halfway up the flank of the dark mountain.

– Ah! Had I not chosen I would
Still choose to assure and shelter them.

*

Where they are, I am.
I will always prevent them.

And whatever looks into their eyes
Will divine their song without ending.

But I will release them. How can I
Deny them the mercy of time?

*

Who watch the crying world wide-eyed,
Without averting their gaze. Who keep

Faith through the fatal night.
Who accept all they think they cannot change

But move when they move with the rhythm
Of purpose. My own children!

*

What opposes grace? Disgrace.
And brutality? Tenderness.

How can hate mother love?
What is the distance from no to yes?

They live in these interstices.
I live in all their choices.

*

Sometimes I think I did not dream it
Entire but only in night's shallows,

And say I have always failed them.
Sometimes I gaze at the curvature

– such shining, such darkness –
And believe that this is still my dream.

*

I watch how they deceive themselves
And deceive one another.

Since they have cast me in their image
They suppose they can deceive me.

And because I have set them free
They cry I have deceived them.

*

They test me with their anguish,
The fearsome hound of their hunger,

Foul diseases that disfigure them,
Worst, their sullen armour of indifference.

I cannot turn away. Like them,
I change nothing. I suffer their suffering.

      *

There is another darker dream
I cannot contain. Is it because

I have chosen not to come close
To them, or because they are not constant,

Or because of their wild beauty,
I trouble myself I am their dream?

Malawi and Norfolk

The Ever-Interesting Topic

by Neil Powell

JOHN SEWELL

Bursting the Clouds

Cape, £8.00
ISBN 0 224 05118 0

WAS IT THE novelist William Cooper who once described sex as "the ever-interesting topic"? His intention would certainly have been ironic, guying a commonly-held misapprehension; yet it's sex that's touted on the back cover of John Sewell's new collection as it also is, in the dubiously encoded form of "raw, dangerous poetry ... a dark, profound, emotional charge", on the jacket flap. After all, sex sells books, even books of poetry, despite the fact that it may not be at all interesting.

What's often of much more interest is the *context* of sex – and that, luckily, is what Sewell's more successful poems are about. The book starts strongly, with 'The Word': it concerns a failing relationship, like much else here, and the speaker's inability to recall the word he'd earlier thought of to sum up the situation; but the occasion of the poem is his partner folding up a travelling table – "The photo on the box has a couple chatting and drinking / at the table on a summer afternoon" – before leaving next day with it and the (presumably, their) kids. The stages of an emotional progress are thus obliquely, and all the more effectively, disclosed through a sequence of mundane, recognisably authentic events. It's a technique which owes something to cinema or to television

drama, in which components of a carefully-placed shot provide keys to a psychological sub-text: so, when the red Peugeot which makes a compromising appearance in 'The Amazing Thing' turns up again, after a minor crunch, in 'The Collision', it's left for the reader to deduce what exactly is going on in the corresponding human lives. In these poems from the book's first section, the bitterness is tangy rather than actually rancid.

Later, the collection becomes more problematical. Writing which is so dependent upon abrupt and often unsatisfactory sexual encounters is bound to run the risk of seeming heartlessly mechanical; and beyond this lies the question of who the "I" who figures in many of the poems may be. Is he the author (in which case one hopes that some other names have been changed, for his friends' sake), or an imagined character, or a shifting mixture of the two? When we read, say, Lowell's marvellous poems of mad destructive passion, we know how they lock into the author's turbulent biography; here, it's impossible to be at all sure. And this matters, because when for instance Sewell writes, in italics which may or may not mean something, "*I fucked her / how she wanted it – hard, with venom*", the reader might wish to know whether the speaker is the author *in propria persona* or a yobbish fiction to be viewed with deserved contempt.

That quotation comes from the sequence wishfully entitled 'Scenes from the Cutting-Room Floor' which concludes the book: most of these poems are of sonnet length, but counting the lines seems to be the only trouble Sewell has taken with his edgily unfinished prosody. They are peopled by individuals called Dave and Liz, Ray and Prue, as well as the unidentified "I" and "He", and they contain occasional allusions which might be intelligible to anyone who knows or cares when 'Madonna Was Number One at the Time' which, incredibly, is the title of a poem. However, there are frustrating moments when it seems as if language is going to be allowed to resonate, as in the first and third lines of 'Martins':

> Beginnings of loss, first fallen swarf of leaves,
> finery and all elation gone. Outside
> the keening of a robin's blade.
> Dulled beat of neighbour hammering on walls.

Here, and at times in 'Rhea's Days by Black Waterfall', one suspects that Sewell's real strengths might be as an altogether calmer, more contemplative sort of poet: when his focus steadies, he has an enviable control of language, and there are better – more interesting – things to be than a fragmentedly versified Martin Amis.

The Shepherd's Sweet Lot

by Gillian Allnutt

ALISON PRYDE

Have We Had Easter Yet?

Peterloo Poets, £7.95
ISBN 1 87147 173 7

ANN DRYSDALE

Gay Science

Peterloo Poets, £7.95
ISBN 1 87147 176 1

THERE'S POETRY IN Alison Pryde's first collection but it's all caught up in the accomplishments of creative writing. I could not, while reading, get out of my mind the image of the writers' group expressing delight and approval at the end of almost every poem. Here is the author of 'Boris' (the tomcat) playing to that particular gallery with a sly and just workable use of cliché:

> He wasn't able to sustain a life
> Of domesticity, but had to leave
> For days or weeks of living on the wild side

Later in the poem is the same author with this:

> He might come back, curl close to them at night,
> Reverberating.

"Reverberating" is right: like Boris, it's "Hunting for food. No one to ask. No one to thank".

There are other bits of language alive among the words. There's the opening of 'Dawn Chorus Line':

> As I walk out on a midwinter morning, hunched
>   and hooded
> In my old, brown anorak, belted with binder twine,
> I have an attendance of birds.

and there's the penultimate verse of 'Bull Fight':

> We patched the fence, cleared up the snap and
>   splinter,
> Bedded each bull, with cows, in his own courting,
> Comfortably settled for the long, dark winter.

Like "attendance", "courting" has an unexpected stateliness. Together with the alliteration, it takes the poem onto another level: here is the barnyard, here also is *Beowulf.*

This, perhaps, is literature absorbed. I loved it so much more than, say, the poems that rewrite some of Shakespeare's GCSE plays – suppose Gertrude betrothed to the other brother at Elsinore, Romeo and Juliet living on into middle age, Shylock become a Christian – or the 'Recycled Poems', though I enjoyed the deadpan plod of "Bird sings. Quite good. / Goes further into wood. / Feel depressive, quite excessive. / Knew I should" and the daft inconsequentiality of "Wish I was back / For the start of the tax year. / I say this, sitting prettily / In Italy".

There are poems in this collection that in no way seek affirmation or applause but speak with an authority of their own. Death is invariably the most stringent writing tutor and Pryde was widowed early. In a poem recording how she and her husband were informed of his terminal illness, she writes:

"This is a play / For which we have not learnt the lines, / And there is no one here to prompt us". ('In Sister's Office, With a Tray of Tea') The following 'Country Funeral' is all hers. It speaks for itself with complete simplicity –

> His cassock flutters in the February wind,
> Thin wind. Slabs of caked earth, green-iced,
> Wait to be fitted back into the ground.

– as does the collection's title poem about her mother with Alzheimer's disease:

> "Who are you?" asks my mother.
> "If you're looking after me
> I ought to know your name."

Only love can be as ordinary, as harrowing as that.

Ann Drysdale

What links these two women poets, unusually, is sheep-farming, Pryde being based at her family farm in Northumberland and Ann Drysdale (I presume) at hers in South Wales. Both insist on the unidyllic realities of rural life, in particular on the hardships of lambing. In 'What Poets Say of Shepherds' Pryde mixes quotes from what I take to be Eighteenth Century pastoral – "O envy the shepherd's sweet lot" – with an account of the birthing of a lamb deformed possibly by the fall-out from Chernobyl. In 'Looking for Lambs' Drysdale curses British Summer Time:

> Damn me for a lousy shepherd. Dark or not
> I should have been here an hour or more ago.

The vigour of these lines is characteristic of many poems in *Gay Science* – a rendering of "*gai saber*", the Provencal name for the art of poetry – and there's nothing whimsical in the humour inform-ing much of the work. Indeed, it is often acerbic –

> The voice of Wales
> Sounds like torn plastic caught in old barbed wire;
> Black tethered tongues desultorily flapping
> ('South Wales, Singing')

– and in 'Language Difficulty' it's exasperated:

> English has words. Ten times as many words
> As there are things for them to be names for.
> In Welsh it's more a case of things per word

In 'A Cold Night on the Wall' it's reckless:

> "Bugger Brigantia! I've had enough
> Of bloody Celts."

Thus Brutus, wine-befuddled Roman soldier waiting for his turn on guard-duty, wrecking the wash-house floor, "Methodically winkling-out and flicking / The little tesserae ..."

Drysdale's book, a second collection, is more even than Pryde's. What it lacks in jewel-like moments, it makes up for with greater verve and confidence. There's a similar experimenting with a wide range of form and subject-matter – work in both collections covers childhood and youth, farm life, pets, marriage, illness, reading matter – but Drysdale is a more discursive poet, arguing some-times with herself ('Poem for Christopher'), some-times with another (as with "Jane B." in 'The Stainless Child'), sometimes with the world with its pollution of dark and silence ('Small Farm at the Edge of Town') and its uPVC values:

> Slowly we lower our sights. Now we demand
> Not that our buildings outlast us as monuments
> To our own lives and the greater glory of God,
> But that they see
> Us
> Out.
>
> ('Unplasticised Polyvinyl Chloride')

Underlying the anger, though, there is much affection here, for friends – "Two people effortlessly holding shares / In one another, like the two of you" is from 'Villanelle for Two Friends' — and for a solid-sounding marriage based partly on a mutual love of crosswords. The last dozen or so poems are concerned with her husband's hospitalisation and a courageous tenderness emerges:

> The stink of Scutari hangs in the still air
> And rises as you shift your thighs in sleep.
> You have been dealt too many wounds, my love,
> And they are weeping in the dark.
> ('Smell. 2')

As Fleur Adcock has noted, women poets may enter the publishers' lists at any age. I, for one, am glad to see collections by two such writers whose best work is grounded in relatively long, thoughtful and well-tempered living.

ROS BARBER

WELL

What I remember most was the white intensity
of your scream. We still tickled then, not too old
at seventeen. Your hair waved shamelessly;
elemental energy seeped through your skin as though
through fissures in a cooling mantle. You were
beyond belief, and words flooded my mouth
like grief as the drowning current of your laughter
swept me away. All this time I've missed you.

He works hard, you sigh, shaking your straight hair still.
Before your first child arrived, he'd capped the spring
and watched it dry. Marshy ground, he says, and a shrill
or social mother, are three of the most insidious things.
It's a family business now, he markets the water
while you man the phone and take orders. Your daughters'
chalky faces on the label make it sell and seem
like a litre of your purity for one pound nineteen.

You were my idol. On a field trip to Bradwell
all our kids ago we catalogued crabs and seaweed
from the nuclear heated streams that fed the beach.
We wrestled in the rancid estuary mud: strange fish
mutated from mermaids hewn from women. Our
laughter shrieked curlews and oystercatchers into
the arms of Essex sky. You were stronger then
than even the tide flooding the scars of our footsteps.

Potato-printed crabs and starfish cover your kitchen,
limpet the fridge. Your elastic daughters are threading
shells of irridescent plastic into necklaces; itching
their eczema absently. Over the sink, a formal wedding
photograph parades you as you used to be. Leave him,
I want to say, as you flake your scalp and briefly scold
your dessicated children. Be wild, be fatal, be cold,
wash him away, I pray, under the hush of your breathing.

Moving and Shaking

By Brian Henry

FREDERICK SEIDEL

Going Fast

Farrar, Straus & Giroux, $20.99

ISBN 0 37416 488 6

BECAUSE SOCIAL CRITICISM in poetry is more often sanctimonious than salutary, a poet as insightful, adventurous, and unsettling as Frederick Seidel is necessary if not entirely welcome. With late-capitalist America as his primary target, Seidel takes aim at the preposterous and the pretentious, scoring points for including himself within his line of sight (he is, after all, a product of the system he scorns). In his fifth collection, *Going Fast*, he continues to play the role of the not-so-idle idler, a wealthy man with expensive tastes and things on his mind. Seidel's persona in these poems flies in First, rubs shoulders with politicians, writes movie scripts, and knows the difference between the Lobb in Paris and the Lobb in London. In 'Racine', he has a Ducati 916 custom-made by "the best mechanics in the world I moonlighting for me after racing hours", and he lets loose on the throttle in "Milan":

> I hiss like an arrow
> Through the air,
> On my way from here to there.
> I am a man I used to know.
> I am the arrow and the bow.
>
> ...
>
> The Stradivarius
> Of motorcycles lights up Via Borgospesso...

Because few people know what a Ducati 916 is, much less who makes it or how it compares to other luxury motorcycles, such information might seem like snobbish rodomontade. But Seidel seems to have created an alternate world for these poems where he is more Don Quixote than Don Juan: "The advice of my physician / Is turn sixty. / I limit lovemaking to one position, / Mounted on a Ducati, monopasto..." This book offers not Seidel's actual world, but satirical and fantastic versions of it.

The result is a collection of poems that seem more wishful than autobiographical, especially when Seidel introduces politics into his Ducati dream sequence, 'Going Fast':

> I see an audience of applause.
> Pairs of hands in rows.
> Palestinian and Jew.
> . . .And Rabin is calling Arafat.
> Arafat, Rabin.

He then roars on his Ducati to President Assad of Syria, "wails straight / To the Wailing Wall", and "walks down the aisle / At a hundred and forty-one miles an hour / To kiss the Torah". Such references shed boyish posturing and acquire a more serious note in the second and sixth sections of the poem – 'Candle Made from Fat' and 'Killing Hitler'. in which "How to keep killing Hitler / Is the point". It would be easy to take Seidel at his word and therefore mistake his persona as just another name-dropping, self-important socialite, as at least one critic has done (William Logan, in *The New Criterion*, calls Seidel's brandishing of privilege a "vulgar display"). But to read Seidel so earnestly – to view him as a rich man trying nonetheless to be a good man – is to outrageously misread him. If these poems are not dramatic monologues, they at least make use of various personae, one of which just might be the wealthy screenwriter readers like Logan will love to despise. Seidelel's poems dare us to believe in his wealth, and they dare us not to hate him for it. But when the poet's "tiny Pitts /... Brightly painted so it can be seen easily / By the aerobatics judges on the ground" is really an "invisible biplane / Parked on display in my living room", we can be excused for excusing his excesses as the products of imagination. In Seidel's poems, after all, "the sky is my living room.

Seidel seems more interested in skewering the vapid and vacuous rich than in joining them, and he revels in uncovering the electroplating on the gold of the glitterati: "The well-dressed man, / The vein of gold that seems inexhaustible, / Is a sunstream of urine on its way to the toilet bowl". While a number of poems in *Going Fast* assault the ramparts of political correctness, others illuminate the complexity inherent in talking about race relations and class differences. 'Mood Indigo' (a title that serves many purposes: the name of a type of fuchsia; of a Frank Sinatra song; of Duke Ellington, Frank Morgan, and Dakota Suite songs and records; and of a Charlotte Vale Allen crime novel whose main character is a movie script doctor) here becomes the rich man's blues. Narrated by a white man robbed and tortured by two black men ("One was blacker"), the poem is harrowing. Because the narrator emerges as racist, we are divided between condemning the loathesomeness of language such as "He find the biggest knife he can / An stab this white boy pretty good / An never even break the skin", no less despicable for its use of a third-person narrative, and condemning the savagery of the torture itself. Seidel declines to solve our dilemma and ends the poem where it begins, *in medias res.*

Like 'Mood Indigo', many of these poems are intended to disturb, upset, and question us and our expectations of poetry. By examining the fabric of moral decisions, Seidel forces us to assess their validity. If his sordid topics – matricide, incest, sado-masochism, torture, masturbation, robbery – seem unremarkable in the current climate of talk-show poetry and post-confessionalism, his satiric, icono-clastic approach invigorates his subject matter, as does the speed of his verse: his rapid-fire rhythms guarantee his poems are never prosaic or dull. Unafraid of being unacceptable, Seidel emerges as an oddity, one of the rare poets who, in a retelling of a tale from Ovid's *Metamorphoses*, can say "Fuck the muse" and still sing.

Transposed Lives

by Paula Burnett

KWAME DAWES

Shook Foil

Peepal Tree, £6.99
ISBN 1 90071 514 7

TARIQ LATIF

The Minister's Garden

Arc, £6.95
ISBN 1 90007 204 1

MAHENDRA SOLANKI

What You Leave Behind

Blackwater, £7
ISBN 0 95285 570 4

THE PECULIAR BLEND of cross-cultural richness and pain which Moniza Alvi calls having a country at your shoulder marks these three collections. They spring from lives now lived in the north – Kwame Dawes in the USA, Tariq Latif and Mahendra Solanki in Britain – but in a sharply tingling sense lived elsewhere at the same time, connected to other places, other times, by tangles of nerves which can register ecstasy as well as jangling. When Dawes writes from his Ghana-born Jamaican experience of America, Latif from his Pakistani-Mancunian perspective, Solanki from the

kind of Britishness which comes from India via Kenya, they are not marginal to the societies in which they now live, love, work and raise their children, but central to what it means to be British or American at the end of the twentieth century.

Kwame Dawes, a major new Caribbean poet, of "prodigious talents" according to David Dabydeen, is preoccupied with dimensions beyond the visible. The Gerard Manley Hopkins echo in *Shook Foil*, his sixth book of verse, suggests an intense devo-tional quality, in tension with the subtitle, 'Reggae Poems'. Yet reggae and Hopkins have spirituality and orality in common. Dawes, reggae-singer-cum-English-professor (and now reggae-poem antholo-gist, too), is indeed a religious poet, but relates otherworldliness firmly to the here and now. His new volume is a tribute to Bob Marley as cultural icon, sufferer, and neglected visionary. A binary rhetoric contrasting the way of the soul with the way of the flesh has been used by Dawes before, but the reggae focus is new, although heralded earlier. In *Prophets* he wrote, "I am turning to the old songs. Marley's call / from the darkness is pure light and hope / despite the countless dead by unbelief". *Shook Foil* visits both the spiritual dimension of reggae and its sensually oriented dancehall culture, with some skilful evocations of the heat of beat and bodies dancing, "the way steady hands / curve round a sweat-smooth waistline, / guiding the rub, the dub, so ready". "Chekeh" is the word used to evoke reggae's "bop / to the off-beat", seen as symbolizing the quest for black identity, for a place in the world, "finding spaces / in the old scores / to build our homes, temples and dreams". But despite the allusions the raw political energy of seventies' dub poetry is lacking, while the portentous Biblical tone at times is strained. There are memorable images, such as "My old lovers / will find their love in sheaves / in dank places", but the energy of the unexpected evaporates in the following cliché about "wading / through old streams of nostalgic / syrup". Some of the work here has a powerful and distinctive voice, but it is not Dawes' best book, perhaps understandably, as his sixth in four years.

Tariq Latif

Tariq Latif's second collection *The Minister's Garden* is particularly eloquent about the cultural pluralism of modern Britain. Its best works deserve to become classics. For these too are poems about identity, or rather identities, in a world characterised by mobility, growth, interaction and hybridisation. Latif has a painter's eye for surfaces and a scientist's eye for inner truths (he graduated in physics). The result is a new kind of metaphysics. He contemplates the manifest and the latent around him, in landscapes and weathers as well as social rites and intensely personal interactions. Interface is the mystery. In front of a landscape of sea and sky he is fascinated by the point at which wave and wind meet, where "Molecules of water and air kiss and couple". On a steamy bus in Valletta rain ("Manchester weather" to go with his "Mancunian English") a Maltese child draws tiny hearts on the window which he embraces with a palm-print, "Something of me in an ocean of mist". In the family living-room the television documentary's window on the Ganges is balanced with the actual window's image of sycamore and street, the pane reflecting simultaneously the silhouette of his parents. Out of sight behind him is the family's reality, youngsters building a western life, but one grounded by their parents in Islamic tradition.

The pain of the senior generation is vividly recorded in these poems. A mother's grief when her son announces he is to take his wife to England makes an iconic scene round the grindstone in 'The Chucky'. The social history is also technological. Where grandmother's muscles turned the chucky, "My mother / Has a Philips grinder and my sister / knows how to change the fuse". Twin metaphors of grafting make a small masterpiece of 'Uncle Jalil', marking both the strain of cultural displacement and the glory of innovation. The surgery on an uncle's "tired heart", by-passed with veins from his legs, is mirrored in the grafting of his orchard, with one tree bearing "Pink, red and white blossoms; British pippin; / American grepner and Turkish

tasha apples". In another poem, father and son tinker with wiring, both with "faith // In electronic diagrams... and / Something beyond". It is the latter which clings obstinately to the science graduate, despite his ignorance of the Koran. When the technology fails, both "Go back to the diagrams / Running short of ideas and / Hope, but with our faiths open / Unshaken and connected". Latif is developing a sure touch.

Mahendra Solanki

Mahendra Solanki's *What You Leave Behind*, his second collection, is briefer, denser than Latif's, and angrier, though in other ways it charts a similar story. Familial relationships are central here too, with the first section focused on leaving home and on the poet's mother, the second on the emotionally complex reaction to the death of the father, and the third on the world built by the speaker – on his relationships as partner and father. The title's suggestion of migration as loss is balanced by gains, as in Latif's work. A spare, stripped poetics delivers the cultural crossings here, sharp with the truth of adaptation, improvisation and reconciliation. There is maternal distress at a son's migration, but also filial trauma at the hands of a feared father who "maimed and hurt across three continents", the son finding his father's face increasingly in the mirror. In these poems leaving is unmistakably escape. The paternal ghost is finally laid, the eldest son's role in a Hindu funeral adapted to new circumstances. Rites are "rehearsed with aunts" but innovation is a saving grace, as is a new "tenderness" towards the dead father, the "old anger long dissipated", like the ashes finally cast eloquently into the river Severn.

Now, like Latif and Dawes, Solanki has his own children, and has learned to replace fear with trust – although 'Blindfold: Exercises in Trust' scrapes the nerves with its images: "You taste of wet grass / your body is bruised like a wall". Some strikingly beautiful love poems form the climax, the more moving for the sense of how hard-won such self-surrender is, "My sharp edges / weathered by your grace". In the end hatred is overcome by compassionate understanding, and the pain of the past by an open future. India is claimed ultimately, in a complex moment of ambiguous identification. Here, as with the other two poets, what remains is a creative ambivalence accommodating the mysterious, multi-faceted nature of things, the reader invited, like the temple-visitor, to "look at the images cut / Out of stone, with your eyes shut".

Reasons to be Cheerful

by Stephen Troussé

FRANCIS PONGE

Selected Poems

Edited by Margaret Guiton
Translated by Margaret Guiton,
John Montague, C. K. Williams
Faber, £9.99
ISBN 0 571 19402 8

TEN YEARS AFTER the author's death, the publication by Faber of a selection of the poetic-prose pieces – *proêmes* – of Francis Ponge is an occasion for the sky to be darkened with hats in the air. Like Clarice Lispector or Donald Barthelme, Ponge has sometimes seemed to be one of those writers of striking singularity who wind up shrouded in commentary and filed away in the more forbidding cloisters of academia. In his own time, Ponge was garlanded with the philosophical mothballs of surrealism, existentialism, absurdism and post-structuralism. I myself first encountered him being given a particularly brutal going-over by Jacques Derrida. It's a testament to the artful fabrication of his word-webs that Ponge continues to ensnare without ever being entirely disentangled. These sparkling translations, of pieces written over four decades, should ensure that this magician of twentieth century letters continues to attract the new readers he deserves.

Born in the last year of the nineteenth century, Ponge grew up to be the kind of youthful *enragé* who might have easily found a home among the anti-aesthetes of the Cabaret Voltaire. As late as 1929 he would write that his project was not a "question of cleaning the walls of the Augean stable, but painting the walls with its own shit". However, by the 'thirties, he had thought himself round to a more affirmative art. George Grosz entitled his memoires of the Dada years *A Big 'No' and a Little 'Yes'*, and it was Ponge's achievement to create his work within the confines of this "little Yes". As he himself remarked, "All poems should bear the title 'Reasons for Living Happily'".

Choosing to "side with things", Ponge found his subject in the domestic, the mundane, the things to hand. And he found his style – a patient, amused, batty, professorial tone – in the French primary school writing exercise of *leçons de choses* (lessons in things) where children are encouraged to describe an ordinary object or creature from both a scientific and literary point of view. This prince of the quotidian writes with neither the homely sentimentality of Neruda's *Odas Elementales*, nor the nerveless detachment of the *nouveau roman*. Rather, he seems to come out of a native tradition of humble enquiry, which might lead from the enlightened scepticism of Montaigne, the encyclopaedic enthusiasms of Rabelais, through Flaubert's Bouvard and Pécuchet to the pataphysical prestidigitation of Alfred Jarry. Like Klee, with whom he has a thing or two in common, Ponge takes his line for a walk... around stoves, blackberries, cigarettes and pigeons.

Writing in concentrated bursts of prose, most often no more than a page, Ponge finds the marvellous in the mundane. Opening an oyster he discovers "the heavens above sinking onto the heavens below form a mere puddle, a viscous, greenish sack fringed with blackish lace that ebbs and flows in your eyes and nostrils". He has a tremendous facility for precise observation, is full of fantastic detail and transformative metaphor. A horse is an "impetuous, spirited chest of drawers", its dung an "omelette" or "brioche of straw, of earth, of rum flavoured from urine". Considering a pebble, he could almost be fulfilling the formalist program of defamiliarisation, of making the stone *stoney*. Except, beyond the linguistic pyrotechnics, Ponge is a writer concerned with formulating an ethics. His meditation on the pebble takes him back through an antediluvian cosmogony, finally paying tribute to the stoicism of these "mute spectators of the blind forces that chase all things beyond reason". A piece about squeezing an orange is at the same time a parable of resisting oppression. It's in this sense that Ponge has sometimes been seen as composing just-so stories for semioticians, fables for phenomenologists. A whole sequence is devoted to the heroism and artistry of molluscs. For Ponge, the molluscs' shells are an "intrinsic part of their being", and also "a work of art, a monument. It endures longer than they do". The mollusc is attached to its shell, just as as the human body is attached to language. Snails, shellfish, crabs, are, if we could but see, saints and examples, making works of art of their lives "of their self-perfecting". Compare this to the banality of trees, endlessly expressing the same old leaf, or the immobile supplication of plants. Ponge's highest hope for his shell of writing is that might endure beyond his own time, and perhaps again be inhabited "as is the case with the hermit crab".

I could conclude this piece simply with recommendations and citations... his celebration of "the pleasures of the door", the wonderful allegory of the lizard, the investigation into the "Nuptial Habits of Dogs", the swallow, the spiders, the frog.... But I would finally like to celebrate Ponge as a supreme comedian. This selection concludes with "...Just Wind!", a piece published after the author's death. It rails against the wind we all know, which considers it an achievement as it "bullies vegetation". It is the moralizing, platitudinous, self-assured "divine afflatus" of the "word-mongers, the windbags". "Oh! If only there were a big guffaw", writes Ponge, "a great wave of hilarity, a fit of convulsive laughter now and then: a *vis comica!* But no".

IAN PARKS
SHELL ISLAND

The girl is tall
and never thinks of food
unless he brings her
oysters from the bay
arranged with lemon
on an oval plate.

It is their only
luxury. At night
an oil-lamp swings
above the bed;
an oval mirror glints
across the hall;

their furniture is sanded
to a cool, transparent sheen.
Incomers, they begin
to feel at home.
Their new republic
is a state of mind

in which the world
of commerce lays no claim.
It has its laws,
its languages – a grove
of olives where
the freed bird sings.

The shells of all
the oceans gather here:
a cache of pink
exotic coils, banked up
against the winter tide.
I ask if it's still possible,

this pool of dreams
and solitudes
in which the driftwood
floats at rest
and lives retract,
becoming simplified.

Across the bay
the new refinery
lights up their hemisphere;
a still white centre
pulses and dilates.
Complex, entire,

it holds their
studied gaze: as alien,
cold and insecure
as the force it draws
its power from,
the city it anticipates.

NEWS/COMMENT

END OF AN ERA

Miroslav Holub and Zbigniew Herbert, two giants of East European and world poetry, died within a fortnight of each other in July. In Holub's case it was completely unexpected: he had been working as hard as ever and although he had suffered health problems in recent years they were not life-threatening. Miroslav was a good friend to the *Review*, its editor, and to the Poetry Society. He never turned down a commission and was always a fount of information and wisdom on every subject under the sun, as his prolific work testifies. He was in touch with the *Review* only weeks before his death, by email. He opened his message: "It's always good to know the electrons work well". He was, as Al Alvarez has said, one of the sanest voices of our time, with a unique and immensely fertile stance on art, history and science and the relations between them.

Zbigniew Herbert was one of the great four of post-war Polish poetry, along with Miłosz, Różewicz and Szymborska. He was the most outspokenly anti-communist of the poets and his 'Damastes (also known as Procrustes) Speaks' remains the most succinct critique of the actually existing communism of Eastern Europe. The next issue of *Poetry Review* will feature tributes to both poets in the context of an issue which begins a survey of poetry in the 20th century in the context of the great events of the time, which will continue through 1999.

ALDEBURGH '98

The Aldeburgh Poetry Festival is the most significant poetry-only festival outside London. Now in its tenth year, it has stuck to its principles and grown steadily, winning plaudits from performers and audience alike. With average audiences of over 200, the feel-good factor, often missing from poetry readings, is there in abundance. This year's bill includes Simon Armitage, Kathleen Jamie, Kwame Dawes, Matthew Sweeney, Sophie Hannah, Rita Ann Higgins, Kevin Crossley-Holland, and Helen Dunmore. The programme copy is also thoughtful and genuinely inspiring. The Festival runs from 6-8 November. The leaflet is included with mailed copies of this issue of the *Review*. For further copies send an SAE to: Poetry Box Office, Aldeburgh Productions, High Street, Aldeburgh, Suffolk IP15 5AX. Box Office: 01728 453543.

FORWARD '99

National Poetry Day, which takes place on October 8, is the backdrop for the Nation's biggest poetry prize: the Forward. This year's contenders are:

Best Collection (£10,000): Anne Carson, *Glass and God* (Cape), Ted Hughes, *Birthday Letters* (Faber), Gwyneth Lewis, *Zero Gravity* (Bloodaxe), Derek Mahon, *The Yellow Book* (Gallery), Glyn Maxwell, *The Breakage* (Faber).

First Collection (£5,000): Olivia Byard, *From a Benediction* (Peterloo), Sarah Corbett, *The red wardrobe* (Seren), Paul Farley, *The Boy from the Chemist is here to see you* (Picador), Jean Sprackland, *Tatoos for Mothers Day* (Spike), David Wheatley, *Thirst* (Gallery).

Best Single Poem (£1,000): Douglas Dunn, 'A European Dream' *(TLS)*, Paul Muldoon, 'Aftermath' (*Sunday Times*), Peter Porter, 'Basta Sangue' *(TLS)*, Sheenagh Pugh, 'Envying Owen Beattie' (*New Welsh Review*), Lesley Saunders, 'The Uses of Greek' (*The Rialto*).

The winners will be announced, and *The Forward Book of Poetry 1999* published, on Wednesday 7 October.

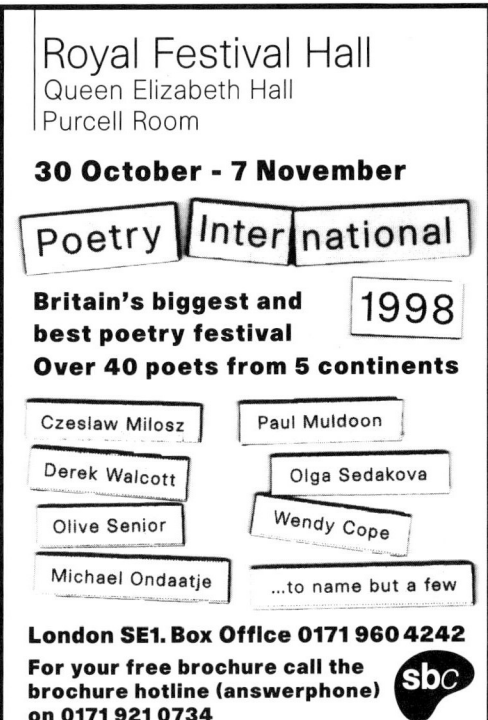

NET VERSE

It takes perseverance to hack your way through the forest of pop-up windows, virtual watermarks and banner advertisements that obscure Geocities sites these days, and find the content beneath the hard sell. Occasionally it's worth the effort. John Kinsella has such a site at **http://www.geocities.com /SoHo/Square/8574/** which has samples of his poetry, poems written in collaboration with other poets, and other experiments. Some of the sections are marked as being under construction, so I'm looking forward to seeing what he adds.

trAce is an online writing community project based at Nottingham Trent University, but with contributors from around the world. They have an ambitious programme of discussions, journals, workshops and so on. Find out more from their site at **http://trace.ntu.ac.uk/**

It was from the trAce site that I found the remarkable GRAMMATRON hypertext at **http://www.grammatron.com/** constructed by Mark Amerika. Whether it's poetry or not I'm not sure, but it's certainly intriguing, and there's a lot of it to explore. You'll need a souped-up browser to make the most of it, since it relies heavily on graphics, and uses RealAudio sound files.

Less demanding of technology, but very useful and welcome is the site at **http://www.netkonect. co.uk/~athelstan/index.htm** from the Blue Nose Poets. This has details of their competition and events, together with some poems from the Blue Nose poets Sue Hubbard and Mario Petrucci.

Lies People Tell is not specifically a poetry site, but it's entertaining and has some interesting poems on the subject of lies, and the effects of lies and lying. If you want to find out what South American parents tell their children will happen if they swallow chewing gum, point your browser to **http://www.liespeopletell.com/**

Tell me nothing but the truth about interesting poetry sites you encounter, by sending email to the usual address:**peter@hphoward.demon.co.uk**

THE INDIAN KING

Jon Silkin had a long association with The Indian King Arts Centre in North Cornwall both as a tutor and as a friend. To celebrate his life and work, the Centre is inaugurating an annual residency for three poets for two weeks from the end of November. For further information, contact Helen Wood at The Indian King Arts Centre, Fore Street, Camelford, Cornwall PL32 9PG, or call 01840 212111.

LETTERS

CONTRA HOLLAND

Dear Peter,

I am puzzled by Jane Holland's remark (*PR* Vol 88, No 2, p53) that "there are too many people out there writing poetry".

Firstly, it surely ill becomes a new poet whose first collection is just out to urge her contemporaries to "rein in their egos" and stop writing poetry for a few years.

Secondly, it begs the question, too many for what? And for whom? Too many to read? Too many to review? Are there too many people out there making chairs or hats or flower-pots or tea-towels or bread, or is it just poems that have a maximum limit? Complaining that there are too many poems is like saying that there are too many sardine sandwiches in the world. You don't have to eat them. What's the problem Jane?

Thirdly, it sounds rather like a complaint that there is too much competition for reviewing space, prizes and critical attention, like saying that there are too many people breathing my oxygen. If Jane really believes that there are too many poems in circulation, why is her second collection coming out so soon?

Finally, it is, to say the least, an unfortunate comment in a magazine which prides itself on leading a poetry revival. So long as someone somewhere needs to reach for the heightened form of expression that is poetry, how can there ever be "too many" poems? Or is the poetry revival only about increasing sales for poets with publishing contracts and reviewing space in *Poetry Review*?

Yours sincerely,
ANDY CROFT
Middlesborough

Dear Editor,

It is clear that Jane Holland has read the title – *Birth of the Owl Butterflies* – of the collection by Ruth Sharman she reviews in your summer issue. Otherwise she would hardly refer to these sometimes chilling poems – one of which, according to the acknowledgments, has been published in *The Faber Book of Murder* – as "very much an exercise in flora-and-fauna poetry".

But it is far from clear whether Jane Holland has read further. The degree of her incomprehension of 'For Joy', the poem she discusses at most length, is remarkable. How can Holland see even the slightest likeness between Plath's 'Daddy' – that over-rated and self-indulgent expression of hatred for the father – and Sharman's calm, if somewhat surprised, recognition of love for the father?

And how can Holland refer to the beautiful last lines of this poem as "prosy"?

> and when I ask you
> why a Green Fritillary
> with just three weeks to fly
> should choose this windy hillside
> high above the sea,
> your answer makes me glad
> to be my father's daughter.

This is far from the language of prose. The line endings enact both the hesitancy of the daughter's question and the slight puzzlement, perhaps even reluctance, with which she takes in the answer. The phrase "my father's daughter", in any other context an awkward circumlocution, further emphasizes the element of surprise in this recognition of kinship. The father's answer is all the more resonant for being absent from the body of the poem; we have to guess that it has been given us in the title. It is almost as if this joy – the poet's as well as the butterfly's – is too great to be more than hinted at.

These lines are neither "prosy", nor merely "pretty". Nor is Sharman merely "managing a meaningful note" – to quote another curiously patronising phrase of Holland's. I hope Holland has given greater attention to the other volumes she reviews than she has to *Birth of the Owl Butterflies*.
Yours sincerely
ROB CHANDLER
London W14

Dear Editor
Jane Holland's review of Marita Over's book *Other Lilies* in the last issue of *Poetry Review* makes me wonder whether it is the poems that are Holland's main concern or her wish to maintain her reputation for ruthlessness. It appears that Holland's method is to fix on individual lines which do not pass her intensity test and use them, irrespective of their context in the poem, to justify sweeping criticisms. Not surprisingly then, she fails to see that the second stanza of 'The Watermelon', cannot be taken in isolation and damned as "chopped up prose" because the power of this section is largely in its relation to the previous stanza. It is an extremely daring transition between two very different styles: playful and ambiguous metaphoricity to dramatic colloquial monologue. Marita Over's ability to make the poem a place where the many threads and levels of perception, emotion, image and style are brought together and allowed to interact is one to the features that makes these poems "the real thing" as Alvarez says. For those interested in something beyond the Procrustean brutality of a reviewer with her own axe to grind, go to 'Song for Ali Tiko', 'Other Lilies', 'The Breakfast', 'Passing the Thresholds' – you will find extraordinary sensory images whose acuteness implicitly brings into question the nature of perception and form as the settled and recognisable thing reviewers like Jane Holland would apparently wish for.
Yours
ROBERT FEATHER
Ashford
Kent

Forthcoming issues

Winter

REQUIEM FOR THE 20TH CENTURY

Miroslav Holub and Zbigniew Herbert: tributes by George Szirtes, Elaine Feinstein and others

Scanning the Century: *The Penguin Book of the 20th Century in Poetry*

Keki Daruwalla: Mandelstam's poem against Stalin

Gerda Mayer: Flight to England from Czechoslovakia 1939

Sean O'Brien: *The Deregulated Muse* and *The Firebox*

Poems by Piotr Sommer, Jayanta Mahapatra, Peter Bland, Bartolo Cattafi, Gottfried Benn, Vitezslav Nezval, James Applewhite

POETRY PLACES COMMISSIONS £500 PER POEM

The Poetry Society wishes to commission some longer poems to publish on our website, linking each one to other suitable sites to be found by new readers interested in their subject.

If you have the germ of an idea about a place that matters to you and some thoughts on a way to publish it which would take your work to new audiences we would like to hear from you.

Your place may be a beauty spot or an eyesore, a place in your home or your imagination. We are not looking for easy poems but ones which will inspire new kinds of readership.

To apply for a commission write to **Morag McRae, at The Poetry Society, 22 Betterton Street, London WC2H 9BU**. Please describe your idea and enclose one or two poems which you would like to bring to our attention.

These are **POETRY PLACES** commissions, funded by the 'Arts for Everyone' budget of the Arts Council of England's Lottery Department.
Full details of the opportunities made available to poets through POETRY PLACES are printed in The Poetry Society's quarterly magazine, *Poetry News*.

SOME CONTRIBUTORS

Smita Agarwal's work appears in *Ten Indian Women Poets* (OUP India).

Gillian Allnutt's latest collection is *Nantucket and the Angel* (Bloodaxe).

Ros Barber's poems have been shortlisted in the National and Arvon Poetry Competitions.

Elizabeth Bartlett's *Two Women Dancing: Selected Poems* is published by Bloodaxe.

Paula Burnett edited of *The Penguin Book of Caribbean Verse*.

Harry Clifton's *The Children of Silone* (prose) is forthcoming from Macmillan.

Kevin Crossley-Holland is editing a new *Exeter Book of Riddles* with Lawrence Sail.

Elaine Feinstein's *Selected Poems* are published by Carcanet.

Duncan Forbes's latest collection is *Taking Liberties* (Enitharmon).

John Fuller's *Collected Poems* are published by Chatto.

John Greening's *New and Selected Poems* are due from Rockingham this year.

Philip Gross's new collection is forthcoming from Bloodaxe.

Paul Groves's latest collection is *Menage à Trois* (Seren).

Sophie Hannah's new collection, *Leaving and Leaving You*, will be published by Carcanet next May.

Roy Hattersley's *Buster's Diaries: As Told to Roy Hattersley* was published by Little, Brown in September.

John Hegley's latest collection is *These Were Your Father's* (Arrow).

Brian Henry is an editor of *Verse* magazine.

Paul Henry's third collection, *The Milk Thief*, is published this month by Seren.

Jane Holland's first collection, *The Brief History of a Disreputable Woman*, is published by Bloodaxe.

Matt Holland is organiser of the Swindon Festival of Literature.

Siân Hughes won the TLS/Poems on the Underground Poetry Competition in 1996.

Jenny Joseph's *Selected Poems* are published by Bloodaxe.

David Kennedy's critical book *New Relations* was published by Seren in 1996.

Ian McMillan's new collection, *I Found This Shirt*, is just out from Carcanet.

John Mole's *For the Moment* is forthcoming from Peterloo.

Sheenagh Pugh's latest collection is *Id's Hospit* (Seren).

Simon Rae's biography of W. G. Grace was recently published by Faber.

Deryn Rees-Jones's new collection, *Signs Round a Dead Body* (Seren) is a PBS Winter Special Commendation.

Ann Sansom's first collection, *Romance*, is published by Bloodaxe.

Carole Satyamurti's *Selected Poems* were published by Oxford Poets in September.

Robert Saxton's first collection, *The Promise Clinic*, is published by Enitharmon.

Vernon Scannell's *Collected Poems* are published by Robson Books.

Adam Thorpe's new novel, *Pieces of Light*, was published by Cape in August

David Wheatley's first collection, *Thirst*, was published by Gallery earlier this year.

Gee Williams was a featured New Poet in *Poetry Review* Vol 87 No 2, 1997.

Kit Wright's poems appear in *Penguin Modern Poets* 1.